RUTH PRETTY COOKING
AT SPRINGFIELD

VIKING An imprint of Penguin Books
Published by the Penguin Group
Penguin Books (NZ) Ltd, cnr Rosedale and Airborne Roads, Albany,
Auckland 1310, New Zealand
Penguin Books Ltd, 80 Strand, London, WC2R 0RL, England
Penguin Group (USA) Inc., 375 Hudson Street, New York, NY 10014, United States
Penguin Books Australia Ltd, 250 Camberwell Road, Camberwell,
Victoria 3124, Australia
Penguin Books Canada Ltd, 10 Alcorn Avenue, Toronto, Ontario, Canada M4V 3B2
Penguin Books (South Africa) (Pty) Ltd, 24 Sturdee Avenue, Rosebank,
Johannesburg 2196, South Africa
Penguin Books India (P) Ltd, 11, Community Centre, Panchsheel Park,
New Delhi 110 017, India

Penguin Books Ltd, Registered Offices: 80 Strand, London, WC2R 0RL, England

First published in 2003

1 3 5 7 9 10 8 6 4 2

Designed and typeset by Seven Visual Communications
Prepress by microdot
Printed in China through Bookbuilders

ISBN 0 67 004541 1
A catalogue record for this book is available
from the National Library of New Zealand.

www.penguin.co.nz

RUTH PRETTY COOKING

AT SPRINGFIELD

Photography by Murray Lloyd

VIKING

AN IMPRINT OF PENGUIN BOOKS

CONTENTS

INTRODUCTION

The moment we walked over the bridge and saw the house we were later to call Springfield, Paul and I both knew we wanted it. It was spring and the house had been unoccupied for several years. Wisteria and the clematis known as Old Man's Beard had overrun the garden. This climber, with a delicate perfume and soft white flowers, is a noxious weed, and in this garden some of its trunks were as wide as the oldest camellia trees. Wisteria had also taken

↑ View looking back to Ruth Pretty Catering buildings – the umbrellas are out for staff lunch. The original barn is used to store feed for our cattle. Upstairs there is a totara floor – one day the barn could become bedrooms, a studio or a shop

a hold, and native tree glades had their floors sprinkled with lilac petals. High up in the trees the strands of mauve flowers looked like telegraph wires. A very confident cabbage tree was growing at one corner of the house, and there the paintwork on the house was tinged with green lichen. Apple trees were in blossom around the water tank, and a shed, later to become our guest cottage, had one wall playing hotel to a family of very busy wasps.

It was a long, white, bungalow-style house, more Australian in appearance than a New Zealand villa. A stream ran through the paddocks, which were fenced really close to the house on one side, and there were a few sheep grazing. A mature totara tree, a dining room for coloured parakeets, stood proud. Daffodils were in flower all around the house, and my niece Emma who was with us picked armfuls of them to take home to her mother. We peered through all the windows and knew instantly that we wanted this property. During the following week we talked and dreamed of nothing else.

The house wasn't for sale, but had been several years previously. Through a local lawyer friend, we found out who the agent had been and approached him directly. He said it would not be possible to buy the property but as we liked the area he could show us some others. Paul and I have always used the approach that if someone says they can't help, they only get that one chance. After that, go directly to the top. We contacted Miles Nathan, the owner of the real estate company, who at this stage was not involved in the day-to-day running

↑ St Margaret's Church

A few days later we owned the house even though we had never been inside!

of the offices. He told us he knew the property well because when he was a teenager he dated the owners' daughter and he would be delighted to renew contact with her parents. Twenty-four hours later he phoned to say he had a contract ready for us to sign.

A few days later we owned the house even though we had never been inside. When the interior was fully revealed, we were stunned to find three marble fireplaces and mahogany parquet floors in the living areas. They were bonuses we hadn't counted on.

The next weekend we arranged to meet the owners on site. Their Mercedes was parked on the bridge when we arrived and their companion servant was making cups of tea. Mr Tolhurst pushed the tea aside and opened a stout leather suitcase with crystal flasks of whisky, gin and brandy in it. Bravely I accepted a gin at 10.30 a.m. on a Sunday and was surprised when no splits were offered. He noticed my slowness in sipping and asked if I would like a top-up of water. I was most appreciative and our meeting continued. We learned that the house and two acres we had bought was originally the homestead of a 100-acre dairy farm that had subsequently been developed into horticultural blocks, mainly kiwifruit with some apple and pear orchards. Mr Tolhurst, who was by then aged 88, and his brother

had inherited the dairy farm. Our vendor had never farmed the property as he was a stockbroker in Wellington, and his brother only farmed for a short time many years ago. The farm stayed in the family but was run by a series of farm managers until its subdivision into blocks in the 1970s. Up until then managers and their families had lived in the house.

There were the remains of a ramshackle wooden building at the entrance to the drive. This transpired to be the site of the local blacksmith who had had a thriving business during the late nineteenth century as timber milling flourished in the nearby ranges. Opposite the driveway entrance there was, and still is, an Anglican church called St Margaret's, slightly topsy turvey because it is still on original wooden piles. Today the local community lead by Mrs Bothamley, Mrs Walker, Mrs Blackburn and Mrs Richmond maintain the brassware and provide astounding vases of their garden flowers for heydays and weddings. Shirley Bothamley's white, scented rhododendron in shiny brass vases is a vision to behold.

As our years at Springfield have passed, pieces of the Springfield jigsaw have fallen into place. In the 1930s the Tolhurst family often lent their property to friends from Wellington. One family has since told us they frequently holidayed at the Tolhurst farm and lived in the house for six months while their brother recuperated from tuberculosis. In the 1940s during a flood, a farmhand was drowned attempting to rescue a sheep. His ghost is supposed to be still here, but I haven't seen Mudgeway yet.

When we began alterations at Springfield we discovered wallpaper covered with horses. This was obviously from the period in the 1950s when the farm was run by a manager who had racing connections.

↑ Salvia, Indigo Spires

Otaki was originally a strong dairy-farming community, but also well known among racing circles for stables, and excellent trainers and jockeys.

The room had been papered over again in the late 1960s as part of the plans architect Sir Michael Fowler conceived for the house as the refit for a Tolhurst wedding. Luckily Sir Michael and the Tolhursts had impeccable taste and the fireplaces and floors, windows and door frames, verandahs and entrance foyer installed at this time still reflect this.

And so we continued to work in the city and spend our weekends at Springfield clearing Old Man's Beard and wisteria to bring life back into the garden. We removed paddock fences, and enlisted friends and family to help. I cooked to feed the helpers, and trailer after trailer load of rubbish went to the tip. I was in a place without a demarcated garden, but I could still pick flowers for every room and I stuck

them into jars or old teapots with abandon. We planted a house orchard, and I read and reread all my cookbooks.

By the time we actually moved into Springfield and called it home, I felt totally rejuvenated about produce, plants and cooking. I had spent ten years in a restaurant and had begun to realise that being caught up in the day-to-day mechanics of cooking and running the restaurant meant I had lost, or may not have ever found, a joy of cooking. In Te Horo I could spend a morning visiting people who were intensely passionate about the vegetables or herbs they grew, and I would return with so many vegetables that I had to invite friends to stay for dinner.

Quite soon, and without me even suggesting it, friends, friends of friends or previous associates began to ask me to cook dinner for them in their homes. I started with perhaps a dinner every two weeks, slowly building up by word of mouth to several events in one week. The first wedding I was asked to cater for was in a disused country hall just out of Ohakune, a farming town near the ski slopes of Mt Ruapehu. I flew up sacks of oysters from Bluff to shuck in view of guests and, with my brother John, butterflied quails to cook on barbecues. I prepared lemon tarts for dessert with lemons from our orchard and found a grower who could provide me with thick, long stalks of asparagus picked to my order. Ruth Pretty Catering was under way.

That wedding was fifteen years ago and since then there have been many weddings, and changes, at Springfield. After three years of catering from the house, Paul and I needed our home back so we took the plunge and invested in a purpose-built commercial kitchen. Kiwifruit growing in our area had fallen from fashion and the

kiwifruit and pear block adjacent to our house became available. This gave us the site and all the space we would ever need for the Ruth Pretty Catering kitchen. We now have a 7000-square foot building to cater in, our own bore to provide us with water, and many herbs and salad beds. And I never dreamed we would need a staff carpark, and that on busy days a park would still be difficult to come by.

Springfield, the house, was allowed to blossom again, and in the kitchen orange Formica benches from Sir Michael's renovation were replaced with red granite. The fireplace originally in the master bedroom and the bedroom itself became part of my new kitchen. With the help of architect Gerald Parsonson and designer Elaine Roberts I finally had my dream kitchen.

Springfield is the place I like best to think in, to sleep in, to cook in, and to share with my family and friends.

I hope *Ruth Pretty Cooking at Springfield* will inspire you to feel the same passion and love for produce, plants and flowers, and encourage you to revel in the giving and sharing of good food and wine.

A BIG NIGHT IN

My mother entertained often, but she never used the word 'entertaining'. She would usually invite parents and their children – it may have been Sunday lunch with aunties and cousins to celebrate an aunt's birthday, or perhaps dinner, which we called tea, for visitors from out of town – and would cook roast beef or lamb with trifle or pavlova to finish. By the time I was a teenager, my mother had acquired a recipe for Beef Stroganoff, which she made in an electric frypan, and it seemed like less trouble than a roast. She would also serve a sherry-laden, crushed gingernut, frozen pudding.

My father, his brother, and one of his sisters were very kindly brought up by an aunt and uncle who had no children of their own. When we were children, Aunty Floss would entertain, but it would always be afternoon tea. If it was just us, afternoon tea would be in the dining room; but if there were several families visiting, it would be in the sitting room and served from a trolley. Aunt Floss's speciality was a very high sponge cake layered with mock cream. We all regarded this social occasion as very posh and had to dress in our Sunday best. Aunty had a lavender-coloured bedroom with a very high double bed covered in a mauve, flounced coverlet. On one occasion she took my mother and I into her bedroom to secretly show us the caul (the foetal membrane) that had covered Aunty Floss when she was born. It looked like parchment-coloured, shrivelled skin. Apparently some babies are born with this covering them. It put me off afternoon tea well and truly that day, and whenever I see mock cream now I immediately remember it.

In the early seventies I was studying drama, so it seemed appropriate to be a hippy and wear long dresses and fur coats. These long dresses stood me in good stead as I became involved with friends who had dinner parties, and I viewed my long hippie dresses as hostess skirts in the evening because by this stage they were all the rage.

One couple, Shona and David Flint, who were a few years older than me, cooked religiously from a *Time Life* series of cookbooks they received each month by mail featuring different countries.

Today I still refer to these books as they were excellently researched and written by people with reputable cooking or food-writing careers, or who went on to have them. At Shona and David's dinner parties you could end up with a Russian meal of vodka, borscht and stuffed cabbage or a grand feast from Vienna featuring Veal Prince Orloff and Sachertorte.

One night Shona promised a Swiss menu including knackwurst and smoked pork chops boiled with potatoes. The main course was preceded by the then current rage of streaking. This meant that you took off all your clothes and literally ran somewhere, but it had to be in public. So before dinner all the guests rather tentatively took off their clothes and ran across Glenmore Street, just up from the Botanical Gardens in Wellington, martinis in hand, then returned to the dining table to enjoy the groaning platter of Alpine pleasures in the nude.

When you are invited to dinner parties, it is de rigeur to invite people back, so I began to hold my own dinner parties. In between drama classes I furiously studied the Cordon Bleu Cookery Course and *Australian Women's Weekly* cookbooks. Everywhere you went in those days hostesses served you frozen grapes with tinned Camembert for the compulsory cheese course, a recipe from the *Australian Women's Weekly Dinner Party Cookbook*. The richness of the recipes in both these series, plus the copious amount of spirits consumed before dining, always knocked me out before the main course and then someone else would have to continue with the rest of the dinner.

I had a brief flirtation with my own feeble version of *nouvelle cuisine* and remember frothing some eggs and pouring the foam back into empty eggshells and then topping them with lumpfish caviar. This culinary trend was supposed to be lighter, but I still remember waking up in a heap on the corduroy pouffe at the conclusion of the evening, with a kind guest having taken over the main course and dessert.

Eventually, my sister Anne led me to the Elizabeth David cookbooks and my dinner parties took on a whole new meaning. I had to stay awake until dessert because I couldn't bear to miss out on my all-time favourite pudding recipe. Even today you can't go wrong if you make Elizabeth David's chocolate cake – it is sensationally rich and chocolatey with a crispy exterior and a meltingly fudgelike interior. Back then I read her books avidly and began to understand that food was all about the quality of the produce, and that before you could cook with any sort of understanding, you needed an appreciation of where ingredients originated from and how it was customary to use them. It was several years after absorbing Elizabeth David that it clicked in my brain this was really the way I had been eating since a child, but from a New Zealand cook's point of view. My mother's food was, and still is, utterly tasty and unpretentious, and is always made from seasonal, top quality produce.

Paul and I have been married for twenty years and have always loved entertaining. In fact, on our first date Paul cooked me dinner, playing it very safe with pumpkin soup, roast chicken and chocolate mousse because he felt nervous about having a chef to dinner. Paul will still often cook for just the two of us, but for guests I always cook. We discuss the menu several weeks ahead, and Paul may have an idea of what wine he is hoping to serve if a guest has a special interest in a wine region or in a wine variety. When the guests are particularly interested in wine, we will try to add some surprises to the wine and food matching. And as I am putting the finishing touches to a dish just before serving, Paul always gives me a taste of the wine to follow so I can tweak the dish if I need to complement any nuances in the wine. It may mean adding a squeeze of lime, a knob of butter, a skerrick of balsamic vinegar or some freshly chopped mint to the sauce. Paul, as always, likes to stick to the pre-arranged timeframe. He doesn't want guests with empty glasses but he won't pour the next wine until the appropriate dish is served.

Renovating Springfield gave me the opportunity to thoroughly plan a new kitchen, and I opted for one which incorporated a large dining table with chairs, a fireplace and stove-tops centre stage. I love to cook in front of people, and have everyone sitting where I am cooking so I don't miss out on a thing. And it's always fun when guests offer to help.

There are French doors leading from the kitchen out to a covered deck, and then into the garden, so the barbecue and wood-fired oven in the garden are really an extension of my kitchen.

We have had some wonderful evenings around our kitchen dining table, which seats ten but at a push can accommodate twelve. The evening usually becomes very noisy and hectic, and fortunately we always have guest rooms ready for those who want to stay the night.

On some occasions, and it is usually in winter, I crave a more formal atmosphere. At one end of our sitting-room there is a dining area with a long, wooden, antique table. I branch out sometimes and substitute the country table with a Georgian D-end dining table; it feels very grand. I like to set this table formally with silver, crystal and embroidered white napkins. And if I feel I am missing out on the conversation I can push open the little bench-high doors from the kitchen bench to the sitting-room.

To be totally honest, I love cooking dinner for my friends and having a big night in.

←
Paul and Ellie enjoying a glass of champagne (left)

←←
Locally grown roses (far left, this page)

←←←
Views from the garden and kitchen at Springfield (opposite page)

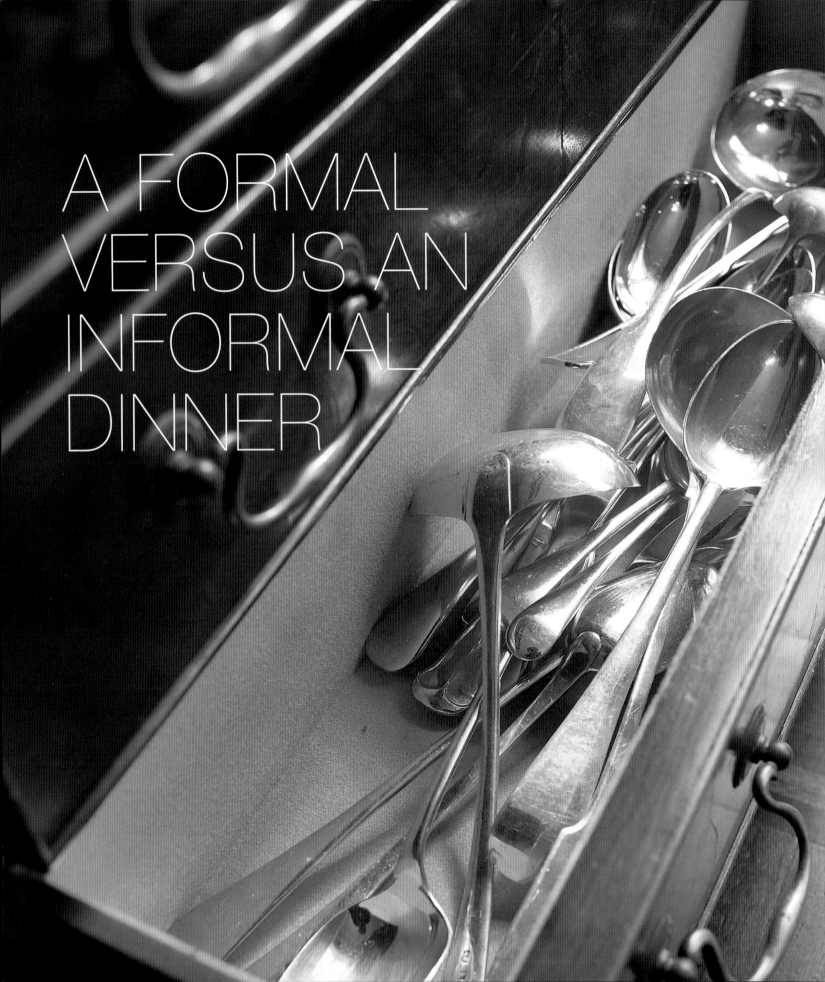

A FORMAL VERSUS AN INFORMAL DINNER

The style of the two dinner menus here is very similar because I don't specifically plan food to be formal or informal. However, for a formal dinner I would not serve lamb shanks or bulbs of roasted garlic as both are too messy. For an informal dinner, I would tend to serve bowls or platters of vegetable accompaniments, whereas for a formal dinner I would devise accompaniments for the meat of the main course. You set the scene for a big night in and guests become the actors in it. The best dinner parties are the ones when the play is unscripted, because, really, it's all about having a social time together with lots of laughs and a shared enjoyment of food, wine and each other's company.

A FORMAL DINNER

Chinese Duck Salad with Wonton Wafers

Parmesan-crumbed Lamb Racks with Mint Pesto

Garlic Potato Cakes, Green Beans with
Lemon-infused Extra Virgin Olive Oil
Oven-roasted Tomatoes

Kapiti Ramaru Cheese with Spiced Nuts,
Preserved Crab Apples and Flowerpot Bread

White Chocolate Raspberry Brittle

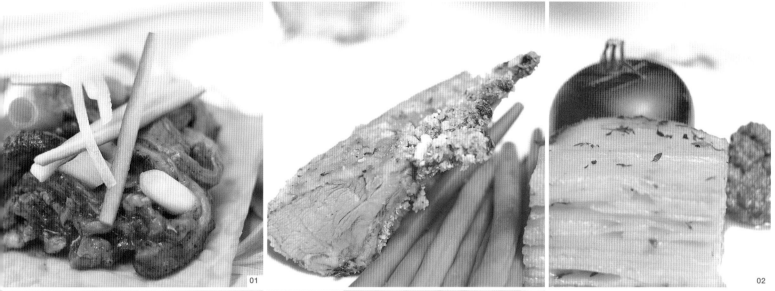

01

03

04

←
Chinese Duck Salad
with Wonton Wafers

Chinese Duck Salad with Wonton Wafers

SERVES 6

Wonton Wafers (see below)

6 handfuls small salad greens
(like rocket or lamb's lettuce)

Chinese Duck Salad (see below)

125g (¼) telegraph cucumber
(cut into thin julienne –
approximately 15mm long)

+ *Duck is great for an entrée as you can begin dinner with red wine. This particular duck dish can be prepared ahead and assembled just as you serve.*

+ Place each Wonton Wafer on a large dinner plate and top with salad greens. Pile Chinese Duck Salad on top of salad greens.

+ Top with julienned cucumber. Serve immediately.

Chinese Duck Salad

SERVES 6 AS AN ENTRÉE

1 tsp finely ground salt

225g (1 double) duck breast

2g (1 tsp) 5-spice powder

100g (5 tblsp) Hoisin sauce

3 spring onions, white part
only (cut on the diagonal)

+ Sprinkle salt on the skin side of duck breast and leave for 8 hours, uncovered, in the refrigerator to draw out the moisture.

+ Wipe dry with a paper towel and rub 5-spice powder into the skin.

+ Preheat oven to 200ºC.

+ Heat a heavy-based frypan and dry-fry duck breast, skin-side down, over medium heat for 5 minutes, until skin is well browned. Pour off fat as it is rendered out of the duck and save for a later use.

+ Transfer duck to a low-sided roasting tray, skin-side up, and cook in oven for 10–15 minutes or until skin is crisp and flesh is cooked medium-rare.

+ Remove from oven and cool.

+ Cut duck breast horizontally through the middle, then cut into thin strips.

+ Just before serving combine with Hoisin sauce and spring onions.

Wonton Wafers

SERVES 6 AS AN ENTRÉE

12 wonton wrappers

125ml (½ cup) sesame oil

+ Preheat oven to 180°C.

+ Lay out wonton wrappers on a large baking tray and lightly brush with sesame oil. Turn the wrappers over and brush the second side with oil.

+ Bake 7–10 minutes or until light golden in colour.

+ Remove from tray and leave to cool.

+ Store in an airtight container for up to two days or freeze for use later.

←

Parmesan-crumbed Lamb Racks with Mint
Pesto, Garlic Potato Cakes, Green Beans
with Lemon-infused Extra Virgin Olive Oil
and Oven-roasted Tomatoes

Parmesan-crumbed Lamb Racks with Mint Pesto

SERVES 4 AS A MAIN COURSE

leaves of winter savory or
thyme, rosemary and
Italian parsley

35g (½ cup) finely grated
Parmesan cheese

70g (1 cup) fresh breadcrumbs

2–4 Frenched New Zealand
lamb racks (trimmed of
silverskin)

70g (½ cup) flour (seasoned)

3 eggs (lightly beaten)

olive oil

Maldon sea salt and freshly
ground pepper

Mint Pesto (see page 24)

+ *New Zealand lamb is admired worldwide and it is possible for the cook at home in New Zealand to purchase lamb racks of the same quality as the finest restaurant in New York might serve. This is exquisite for a big night in.*

+ Chop enough herbs to equal ¼ cup of combined herbs.

+ Mix together herbs, Parmesan and breadcrumbs.

+ Pass lamb racks first through flour, then eggs and then breadcrumb mixture. Refrigerate for at least an hour or overnight.

+ Preheat oven to 220ºC.

+ Spray or brush a low-sided baking tray with olive oil and heat in oven for 5–10 minutes.

+ Place lamb racks on preheated tray, season with salt and pepper, and cook for 12–15 minutes, or until racks are cooked medium-rare.

+ Remove from oven and rest lamb racks in roasting tray covered with a heavy tea towel and away from heat for at least 10 minutes.

+ Carve into single or double cutlets and serve accompanied with Mint Pesto. Double cutlets will ensure the lamb stays hotter.

Mint Pesto

MAKES 425ML

1 cup mint leaves (tightly packed)

125ml (½ cup) lemon juice

150g (1 cup) pinenuts (or any preferred nut)

1½ tsp salt

125ml (½ cup) olive oil

+ *I often make pesto to serve as an accompaniment without cheese or garlic. This way you can truly taste the purity of the herbs and the pesto doesn't overpower other flavours.*

+ Place mint and lemon juice into a bowl of a food processor fitted with a metal blade and quickly process to chop mint.

+ Add pinenuts and salt, and process until well blended. With the motor running, drizzle in olive oil through the feed tube to form a smooth paste.

Garlic Potato Cakes

*MAKES 9 ROUND SERVINGS
OR 12 SQUARE SERVINGS*

2 kg (6–7) large potatoes (preferably Agrias)

100–120g butter (melted)

5 cloves garlic (crushed)

Maldon sea salt and freshly ground black pepper

+ *This is an excellent 'do ahead and reheat' potato dish. For a formal dinner I like to present guests with a completed plate that looks balanced and attractive, rather like a simple version of a restaurant meal.*

+ Preheat oven to 200°C.

+ Peel potatoes and slice very thinly. A mandoline works brilliantly for this job, but if your kitchen doesn't run to this use a Rex peeler or a very sharp knife.

+ Mix butter and garlic. Brush butter mixture over the base and sides of a small roasting dish, 22 x 29cm. Place 2 layers of potatoes in the roasting dish, overlapping slices as you layer. Brush well with butter and season. Repeat layers of potatoes, butter and seasoning until all potato is used. The potatoes should reach just under the rim of the roasting pan.

+ Brush top with butter mixture. Cover gratin with aluminium foil and bake for 1 hour, or until potatoes are soft when pierced with a fork.

+ Remove from oven. Recover with aluminium foil and place a weight on top of potatoes. The weight could be a smaller roasting tray with a couple of cans of baked beans in it. When cool, place in refrigerator and leave for at least 4 hours, but preferably overnight, with the weight on top.

+ When you are ready for dinner, preheat oven to 220°C.

+ Using a 7.5cm round cookie cutter cut potatoes into rounds. If you prefer, cut into squares as this way there is no wastage.

+ Place Garlic Potato Cakes on a greased baking tray and bake for 12–15 minutes or until golden and tops are crispy.

Green Beans with Lemon-infused Extra Virgin Olive Oil

SERVES 10

750g green beans

salt

15ml (1 tblsp) lemon-infused
   extra virgin olive oil

Maldon sea salt and freshly
   ground black pepper

+ *Beans are my favourite vegetable and Sue's Market Garden excels
   in growing beans. Sue will only sell them to me the day they are
   picked.*

+ If beans are the flat variety, I like to slice them using an old-fashioned bean
   slicer so they are as thin as spaghetti. If they are round beans, just trim off
   the ends.

+ Bring a large pot of water to the boil and add a pinch of salt.

+ Plunge beans into boiling water and cook, uncovered, until just past al dente.
   I like my beans touch tender and not crunchy. Drain water immediately.

+ If you are not serving immediately, line a bowl with a cold, wet tea towel,
   place hot (undressed, but drained) beans into the bowl and cover with
   another cold wet tea towel. Beans will remain green and hot for up to
   30 minutes held this way.

+ Just before serving add olive oil and seasoning.

Oven-roasted Tomatoes

SERVES 8

small handful of winter savory
   or thyme

500g (8 medium round)
   tomatoes with calyxes on

45ml (3 tblsp) olive oil

½ tblsp Maldon sea salt

+ *Tomatoes cooked in this fashion provide not only colour to the plate
   but also a natural, sweet and sour sauce to complement the lamb.*

+ Preheat oven to 180ºC. Braise savory or thyme leaves in a mortar and pestle
   or using the side of a chef's knife. Place into a compact roasting tray.

+ Put a cross on bottom end of tomatoes and brush all over with olive oil.

+ Place tomatoes in roasting tray, bottom-side up. Season with salt.

+ Bake for 30 minutes or until tomatoes are soft and skins are just lifting.

←

Kapiti Ramaru Cheese
with Spiced Nuts,
Preserved Crab Apples
and Flowerpot Bread

Spiced Nuts

MAKES 3 CUPS

1 egg white

60g (3 tblsp) honey (runny
   clover)

2 tsp Maldon sea salt

½ tsp chilli powder

2½ tsp cumin powder

1¾ tsp cayenne pepper

½ tsp allspice

½ tsp curry powder

80g (½ cup) peanuts

60g (½ cup) pecan nuts

80g (½ cup) Brazil nuts

75g (½ cup) cashew nuts

80g (½ cup) blanched almonds

+   *In a different context, these nuts become a very good gift for a man as they are positively moreish with a cold beer and look very attractive presented in a large jar. Any favourite combination of nuts can be used, provided you keep the overall quantity at 2½ cups. They are very edible before dinner with champagne, but also a tasty counterbalance to cheese, particularly when served with a cabernet or a pinot noir with spicy overtones.*

+   Preheat oven to 180ºC.

+   Beat egg white until soft and foamy. (When egg white is foamy, no clear liquid will remain on the bottom of the bowl.)

+   Add honey, salt and spices and combine well. Add nuts and stir until well coated.

+   Spread mixture on a tray, preferably lined with a Teflon sheet as honey can burn on the tray.

+   Bake for 15 minutes then remove tray from oven. Toss nuts with a metal spatula, stirring and separating nuts.

+   Reduce oven to 150ºC and return nuts to bake for about 10 minutes until golden brown.

+   Remove nuts from oven, toss and stir again to break up any nuts that are stuck together.

+   Leave to cool. Nuts will crisp up on cooling.

+   Store in an airtight container at room temperature for up to 2 weeks. If the nuts become slightly sticky, then refresh them in the oven, which gives you the added bonus of serving them warm.

Preserved Crab Apples

MAKES 3 1-LITRE JARS + 1 300ML JAR

1.750 litres (7 cups) water
1.4kg (7 cups) sugar
2kg crab apples

+ *I always like to have a few jars of these in my pantry. They look very pretty served as a garnish with a pork or ham dish, and exceptionally glamorous studding a leg of ham. Serve one or two crab apples per person with a creamy white cheese like Brie or Kapiti Ramaru which is a washed-rind cheese. I have even seen guests mush up the interior of the cheese with some of the syrup from the crab apples.*

+ Preheat oven to 130°C.

+ Combine water and sugar in a large pot and stir over a medium heat until sugar is dissolved.

+ Bring to the boil.

+ Tightly pack crab apples into sterilised and still-hot jars.

+ Using a jug, pour hot syrup into the jars to the very top.

+ Cover each jar with aluminium foil and place on a baking tray. Place into oven and cook for 25–30 minutes until crab apples are fork tender but not mushy.

+ Reheat remaining syrup.

+ Remove jars from oven and pour hot syrup into each jar until the jar is overflowing.

+ Seal with sterilised lids.

+ Leave jars to cool, then wash and dry jars. Store crab apples in a cool, dry cupboard.

+ If sealed correctly, Preserved Crab Apples will keep for 8–12 months. Once opened, store in the refrigerator.

Flowerpot Bread

MAKES 15 LITTLE FLOWERPOTS

salad oil for brushing pots

12g (1 tblsp) yeast granules

15g (1½ tblsp) sugar

375ml (1½ cups) lukewarm
   water

630g (4½ cups) flour

10g (2 tsp) salt

125ml (½ cup) salad oil, extra

110g (1 cup) roughly chopped
   walnuts

+ *When I discovered that those cute little terracotta pots were useless
   for plants as they are too small for a plant to gain any nourishment, I
   didn't want to throw them out. They sat there until one day I wanted
   to make a nut bread to accompany cheese. I had read somewhere
   that you could paint terracotta pots with oil and bake bread in them.
   This worked beautifully, and I constantly use them to this day.*

+ To prepare flowerpots, thoroughly brush them with salad oil, inside and out,
   and place in the oven for 15 minutes at 200°C to let oil bake in. This must be
   done when pots are used for the first time. Brush flowerpots with salad oil
   again immediately before using, inside and out, and be generous with the oil.

+ Soften yeast and sugar in water. Cover with plastic wrap and leave for
   10–15 minutes in a warm place until mixture becomes frothy.

+ Place flour and salt in the bowl of an electric mixer. Make a well in the centre
   and pour in yeast/water mixture. Using dough hook, mix dry and
   wet ingredients together. Have the mixer on the lowest speed as the
   dough is thick and it will be heavy going for the mixer.

+ With the electric mixer running, slowly pour in salad oil. Continue mixing
   for about 10 minutes or until dough becomes glossy. The dough should
   hold its shape and come away from the sides of the bowl. With mixer
   still running, add walnuts until they are incorporated into dough.

+ Place dough in a large oiled bowl, then oil top of dough. Cover with plastic
   wrap and leave for approximately 1½ hours in a warm place or until dough
   has doubled in bulk. You can put it on a rack on top of a warm oven or
   beside a sunny window.

+ Divide dough into 15 pieces and form each piece into a ball. Place ball
   between thumb and forefinger. Gently squeeze and pull dough down to
   create a cone shape.

+ Preheat oven to 220°C.

+ Place dough with the pointed end down into the flowerpots and brush
   tops with more oil. Place flowerpots on a baking tray. Cover completely
   with plastic wrap and leave in a warm place to prove until bread rises
   to top of flowerpots. This may take 30–45 minutes.

+ Place in oven and bake until loaves are walnut brown and sound hollow
   when tapped.

+ The bread can be made ahead of time, removed from flowerpots and
   frozen. A few hours before bread is required, return it to flowerpots
   and let thaw naturally.

↑ Our gardener Clare Douglas creates
an everchanging array of potted plants

←
White Chocolate
Raspberry Brittle

White Chocolate Raspberry Brittle

MAKES 32 X 23CM SLAB. CUTS INTO 64 TRIANGLES

300g (1¾ cups) white chocolate buttons (or slab chocolate smashed into small pieces)

90g (¾ cup) frozen raspberries (thawed) or smaller quantity of fresh

+ *I use Belgian chocolate, but if you wish use Milky Bar. Chocolate melts are not suitable for this recipe. This divine little sweet can be kept in the freezer and brought out to complement coffee.*

+ Line a 32 x 23cm low-sided baking tray or a slice tin with a Teflon sheet.

+ Melt chocolate over double boiler, making sure that the water does not touch the bottom of the bowl holding the chocolate. Be careful not to allow the chocolate to become overheated.

+ While chocolate is melting, place raspberries in a food processor fitted with a plastic blade and process briefly. Strain purée through a fine sieve to obtain 30ml (2 tblsp) of raspberry purée.

+ Stir chocolate with a metal spoon until smooth. Using a palette knife (a long, thin metal spatula), spread chocolate over the Teflon sheet.

+ With a spoon, drizzle raspberry purée over white chocolate. Swirl purée into white chocolate, using the blunt end of a skewer or toothpick.

+ Let White Chocolate Raspberry Brittle set at room temperature for approximately 2 hours. Do not be tempted to put it into the refrigerator, as this will cause condensation to form. Turn brittle out, Teflon sheet-side up, onto a large chopping board. Peel Teflon sheet off and cut brittle into desired shapes. The raspberry purée will remain slightly tacky, so handle carefully and do not stack the pieces while at room temperature.

+ Serve White Chocolate Raspberry Brittle immediately. Alternatively, free-flow freeze brittle and once completely set, stack pieces with wax paper in between into an airtight container and freeze for up to 3 months.

AN INFORMAL DINNER

Spiced Yoghurt with Homemade Crackers

Vigneron's Salad

Roast Rack of Ham in Maple Syrup
Marinade with Apricot Relish

Sweet Baked Kumara

Crunchy Green Bean Salad with Cranberries

Rice Pudding with Bruléed Feijoas
and Vanilla Ice-cream

01
Spiced Yoghurt with
Homemade Crackers

02
Vigneron's Salad with
Lemon Dressing

03
Roast Rack of Ham in
Maple Syrup Marinade
with Apricot Relish

04
Sweet Baked Kumara

05
Crunchy Green Bean
Salad with Cranberries

06
Rice Pudding with
Bruléed Feijoas and
Vanilla Ice-cream

→

Spiced Yoghurt with
Homemade Crackers

Spiced Yoghurt with Homemade Crackers

MAKES 310G

500ml natural yoghurt

2 tsp cumin seeds (toasted)

20 mint leaves (finely
   shredded)

2 tblsp finely chopped Italian
   parsley

½ tsp Maldon sea salt

few grinds white pepper

Homemade Crackers
   (see opposite page)

+ *My friend and colleague, Suneeta Vaswani, is an Indian cooking
teacher living in Houston, USA. This is my version of her recipe.
Suneeta always has it in her refrigerator and her family enjoy it
on toast for breakfast.*

+ Place a sieve lined with muslin over a bowl.

+ Pour yoghurt into muslin. Pull the corners of muslin together and
tie up with kitchen string.

+ Leave to sit in refrigerator for 4 hours or overnight.

+ The following day, discard liquid collected in the bowl and transfer
the yoghurt from the muslin to a clean bowl.

+ Place cumin seeds in a mortar with a pestle, or in a spice grinder,
and grind finely. Add to yoghurt.

+ Add herbs and seasonings and combine well.

+ Eat immediately or for an even better flavour leave in refrigerator
until the following day.

Homemade Crackers

+ *Philippa Falloon, who owns a wonderful country house lodge called Bowlands in the Wairarapa, gave me my first taste of homemade crackers, and I was hooked. She served them with pre-lunch drinks with Stilton cheese, almonds and muscatels. They are definitely worth the trouble to make.*

MAKES 70 5CM SQUARE CRACKERS

280g (2 cups) high grade flour

1 tsp salt

2 tsp sugar

20g (2 tblsp) cold unsalted butter (cut into very small dice)

195ml (¾ cup) milk

Maldon sea salt

cumin seeds

+ Preheat oven to 180°C.

+ In a large bowl combine flour, salt, sugar and stir to combine. You can use a food processor but it does result in a tougher finished product.

+ Add butter and combine by rubbing butter into flour and continue until mixture resembles coarse meal.

+ Make a well in the centre of the bowl and pour in milk. Using a knife, gradually combine the flour and milk until the dough comes together to form a soft ball.

+ Cover dough with plastic wrap and allow to relax at room temperature for 15–20 minutes.

+ Unwrap dough, place on a lightly floured surface and roll into a 44cm square, 2mm thick. It is important to roll the dough thin to achieve the desired crispness. If the dough continues to spring back as you roll, allow it to relax again by covering and leaving to sit for a further 15–20 minutes. This is more likely to happen if you have made the mixture in a food processor.

+ Sprinkle dough lightly with salt and gently press it into the dough with a rolling pin.

+ Using a sharp knife, cut dough into 5cm squares. Sprinkle with cumin seeds or make a mixed batch by sprinkling with a variety of seeds or spices, e.g. sesame, caraway, or paprika. Gently press seeds into the dough using a rolling pin.

+ With a thin spatula, lift biscuits to an ungreased baking tray and liberally pierce with a fork.

+ Bake for 20–25 minutes, until lightly browned and crisp. Rotate oven tray if necessary to encourage even cooking.

+ Leave to cool and serve immediately, or store in an airtight container for 1–2 weeks.

→

Vigneron's Salad
with Lemon Herb
Dressing

Vigneron's Salad with Lemon Herb Dressing

SERVES 8

75ml (¼ cup + 1 tblsp) verjuice

90g (½ cup) muscatels (stems removed)

8 large handfuls watercress (washed and stalks removed)

100g (1 cup) walnut halves (toasted)

200g Kapiti Kikorangi cheese (cut into 1cm cubes)

60ml (¼ cup) Lemon Herb Dressing (see below)

+ *A salad is an enticing entrée because it is light and tasty and prepares you for the next course, rather than filling you up. Here I have used verjuice in the dressing to make it compatible with wine, as vinegars are not necessarily wine friendly.*

+ Lightly warm verjuice and pour over muscatels. Leave to sit at room temperature for at least 1 hour. Drain and retain verjuice to use in Lemon Herb Dressing.

+ In a large salad bowl combine muscatels, watercress, walnuts and cheese.

+ Just prior to serving, pour Lemon Herb Dressing over salad and toss gently.

+ Serve immediately.

Lemon Herb Dressing

MAKES 250ML

125ml (½ cup) extra virgin olive oil

65ml (¼ cup) verjuice (drained from muscatels)

1½ tsp finely chopped fennel or dill

1 tblsp chopped Italian parsley

juice and rind of 1 lemon

35g (½ cup) finely grated Parmesan cheese

1 egg (lightly beaten)

½ tsp Maldon sea salt

½ tsp freshly ground black pepper

+ *This dressing resembles a Caesar Salad dressing because the raw egg helps the dressing to adhere to the salad leaves. Try it also drizzled over grilled fish.*

+ Combine all ingredients in a bowl and whisk together with a fork.

+ Store in refrigerator.

Roast Rack of Ham in
Maple Syrup Marinade
with Apricot Relish

Roast Rack of Ham in Maple Syrup Marinade with Apricot Relish

SERVES 6

1.5kg (8 cutlets) ham rack

170g (½ cup) clover honey

30ml (2 tblsp) malt vinegar

Maple Syrup Marinade
(see page 40)

Maple Syrup Jus
(see page 40)

Apricot Relish
(see page 41)

+ *Maurice Taylor, our local butcher, still cures his own hams and bacon, and makes his own pork sausages. A rack of ham is inspirational because you have perfect portion control and it is very quick to cook. Maurice suggests to ask your butcher for a rack of pork, cured and smoked, as opposed to ready to glaze. In this recipe I am starting with a raw ham rack, boiling it to cook, then roasting in the oven to essentially glaze it.*

+ Place ham rack in a large pot of cold water, making sure it is entirely covered.

+ Add honey and vinegar, (adjust measurement according to weight of rack), cover with lid and bring to the boil.

+ Lower heat, adjust lid so it sits half covering the pot, and simmer rack for 1–1¼ hours, or until tender when pierced with a cake skewer. Allow 20–25 mins cooking time per 500g.

+ Remove from heat. Leave ham rack sitting in liquid and when cool place in the refrigerator overnight.

+ The following day remove ham rack from liquid and discard liquid.

+ Carefully cut skin off ham rack, leaving a thick layer of fat covering the meat, and discard. Score the rack by cutting into the fat in diagonal lines to a depth of 1cm and repeat cutting on the opposite diagonal to achieve diamond-shaped cuts.

+ Spread half of Maple Syrup Marinade evenly over rack and marinate at room temperature for 1 hour, or refrigerate for up to 8 hours. Baste ham rack occasionally while marinating.

+ Preheat oven to 170ºC.

+ Line a roasting tray with aluminium foil and place ham rack in base. Tip some marinade from bowl over ham rack.

+ Place ham rack in oven and cook for 45–60 minutes or until tender. During cooking, baste generously with the remaining glaze every 15 minutes.

+ Carve into cutlets, drizzle with Maple Syrup Jus and accompany with Apricot Relish.

Table laid for an informal dinner
in the Springfield kitchen

Maple Syrup Marinade

MAKES 260ML

2 tsp dry mustard powder

½ tsp ground cinnamon

30ml (2 tblsp) cider vinegar

160ml (⅔ cup) maple syrup

40g (3 tblsp) prepared Dijon
     mustard

30ml (2 tblsp) soy sauce

Maldon sea salt and freshly
     ground black pepper

+ *You will need 1 recipe to marinate rack of ham and 1 recipe for Maple Jus.*

+ In small bowl combine dry mustard, cinnamon and vinegar, and mix to a paste.

+ Add maple syrup, Dijon mustard, soy sauce and seasonings, and stir well. It should be spicy but sweet.

Maple Syrup Jus

MAKES 250ML

1 recipe Maple Syrup Marinade

250ml (1 cup) chicken stock

+ Combine Maple Syrup Marinade and stock in a medium-sized pot.

+ Bring to the boil and reduce by half.

→

Apricots ripening at Windsor
Park, a local market garden

Apricot Relish

MAKES 500ML

250g (1¼ cups) sugar

10ml (2 tsp) lemon juice

zest of 1 orange

juice of 2 oranges

260g (1¾ cups) dried apricots

1 medium (190g) apple (peeled
    and diced)

freshly ground white pepper

2 tsp yellow mustard seeds

2 tsp brown mustard seeds

olive oil

30ml (2 tblsp) verjuice

+ *This is a fresh relish, not a preserve, and needs to be stored in the refrigerator where it will keep indefinitely. If there is any left over I love it with celery and Cheddar cheese. Use the plumpest dried apricots you can find. I prefer to use dried apricots either from the Barossa Valley or Otago.*

+ In a small saucepan combine sugar and lemon juice and cook over a medium heat until sugar begins to caramelise. Do not stir.

+ When sugar has reached a golden caramel colour, add orange zest and turn down the heat.

+ After a minute, add orange juice, apricots, apple and pepper, and stir to combine.

+ Continue to cook over a medium heat until the apricots are soft and the relish is thick.

+ While relish is cooking, toast the mustard seeds in a little oil until they just start to pop. Remove from the heat, transfer to a mortar and pestle and crush about half the seeds.

+ When relish has cooled slightly, stir in mustard seeds and verjuice. Refrigerate until ready to use.

+ Serve at room temperature.

→
Sweet Baked
Kumara

Sweet Baked Kumara

*SERVES 6–8 AS AN ACCOMPANIMENT
TO MAIN COURSE*

1 kg (4 medium) golden
   kumara (scrubbed)

Maldon sea salt and freshly
   ground black pepper

½ tsp paprika

30ml (2 tblsp) maple syrup

20g (2 tblsp) butter
   (cut into small dice)

65ml (⅓ cup) apple cider

+ *This way of cooking kumara is particularly tasty with the ham rack. For convenience, I prepare the kumara to the stage of adding the apple cider vinegar up to a day ahead.*

+ Place kumara into a pot of boiling water, reduce heat and simmer until tender when pierced with a knife, about 25 minutes.

+ Drain, cool and peel kumara when able to be handled. Slice lengthwise into quarters.

+ Preheat oven to 180°C. Butter a 28cm oval baking or gratin dish.

+ Place kumara in a single layer in dish. Sprinkle with salt, pepper and paprika, and drizzle with maple syrup. Dot with butter and pour apple cider over kumara.

+ Cover with aluminium foil and roast in oven for 45 minutes, until soft and moist.

+ Add more seasoning to taste if necessary. Serve immediately.

→
Philip Sue picking beans
in his market garden

Crunchy Green Bean Salad with Cranberries

*SERVES 8 AS AN ACCOMPANIMENT
TO MAIN COURSE*

100ml (½ cup + 1 tblsp) fresh
    orange juice

100g (¾ cup) dried cranberries

45ml (3 tblsp) sherry vinegar

2 tblsp Dijon mustard

¾ tsp Maldon sea salt

125ml (½ cup) walnut oil

600g green beans (prepared)

Maldon sea salt and freshly
    ground black pepper

+ *Sherry vinegar, walnut oil and verjuice, once opened, all keep
better if stored in the refrigerator. I like to use dried cranberries
often – they supply an acidic fruity burst which helps to
co-ordinate a dish with red wine and in particular with pinot noir.*

+ In a small pot heat orange juice until warm. Add cranberries and soak for
approximately 5–10 minutes. Drain cranberries, reserving 2 tblsp liquid.

+ In a small bowl whisk together vinegar, mustard and salt. Slowly drizzle in
walnut oil, whisking constantly until mixture is emulsified. Add the reserved
cranberry juice. Set aside.

+ Place beans in a pot of boiling salted water and cook for 3–4 minutes or
until tender. Drain immediately and immerse in iced water. Remove beans
and pat dry. Place in large bowl.

+ Add cranberries and gently toss with the dressing.

+ Season to taste.

Rice Pudding with Bruléed Feijoas
and Vanilla Bean Ice-cream

Rice Pudding with Bruléed Feijoas and Vanilla Bean Ice-cream

SERVES 6

160g (12 tblsp) jasmine rice

60g (6 tblsp) sugar

600ml (2 cups + ⅓ cup +
    1 tblsp) milk

120ml (½ cup less 1 tsp) cream

seeds from 1 vanilla bean

freshly grated nutmeg

Bruléed Feijoas (see opposite
    page)

Vanilla Bean Ice-cream
    (see page 183)

+ Preheat oven to 140°C.

+ Place 6 ungreased soufflé dishes (8.5cm diameter, 4.5cm depth) in a low-sided baking tray. Place 2 tblsp rice and 1 tblsp sugar in each of the soufflé dishes.

+ Place milk, cream and vanilla bean seeds in a jug and lightly whisk to combine. Pour evenly into soufflé dishes and gently stir to combine ingredients.

+ Sprinkle with freshly grated nutmeg.

+ Bake puddings on the tray, as the liquid is likely to overflow, for 60–65 minutes until rice has absorbed liquid and the tops of the puddings are golden brown.

+ Wipe outside of soufflé dishes and serve while hot or warm with Bruléed Feijoas and Vanilla Bean Ice-cream.

+ Pass around a jug of lightly whipped cream separately if you wish.

Bruléed Feijoas

SERVES 6

600–700g (6) feijoas (cut in half
    lengthwise, peeled if you wish)

12 tsp Brulée Sugar Crystals
    (see below)

+ Preheat oven to 220°C.

+ Place feijoas on a low-sided baking tray and pour in enough cold
    water to just cover the base of the tray.

+ Place tray in oven and bake for 10 minutes or until feijoas are soft
    and yielding.

+ Remove from oven and sprinkle with Brulée Sugar Crystals.

+ Preheat grill. Place tray under grill for 3–4 minutes until Brulée Sugar
    Crystals have melted. Alternatively, melt crystals using a chef's
    brulée torch.

+ Serve hot with Rice Pudding and Vanilla Ice-cream.

Brulée Sugar Crystals

MAKES 1½ CUPS

300g (1½ cups) sugar

150ml (½ cup + 1 tblsp +
    2 tsp) water

+ *An extremely handy addition to any freezer, this was an idea given to
    me by my friend and colleague, Shelley Templer. I use these crystals
    as the sugar on top of Crème Brulée as they melt very quickly,
    ensuring the brulée stays cold underneath. When I gather a few ripe
    figs off the tree, I cut them in half and grill or brulée crystals on them.
    Unlike feijoas, ripe figs do not require cooking first.*

+ Place sugar and water into a pot and stir over a gentle heat until sugar
    is dissolved. Bring to the boil and cook for 5–10 minutes, without stirring,
    until mixture is a pale amber colour.

+ Line a baking tray with a Teflon sheet and pour caramel onto sheet. Leave
    to cool. Once cold, roughly break up and place caramel into bowl of food
    processor fitted with a metal blade. Process just until you have fine crystals.
    Pour crystals into a container and seal tightly. Freeze until required. Freezing
    the mixture stops it sticking together. Brulée Sugar Crystals can be made
    weeks in advance if kept airtight and frozen.

BIRTHDAYS

Paul and I have the good luck, or misfortune, to have our birthdays on the same day, 4 January. The day before, I pack away everything to do with Christmas because when I was a child my birthday was always clouded by Yuletide celebrations. Adults seem to revel in giving joint Christmas and birthday presents, but I could always see through the shortie pyjama Christmas top and the shortie pyjama birthday bottom deal.

The day before our birthdays, we always visit our favourite local growers, including Sue and Gary Walden from the Vege Nook. Because it is the holidays, they always offer us a cold beer and we sit in their backyard and talk about raised herb beds and how they manage the gardens in a sustainable fashion. It's a prolific time of the year for vegetables, and I spend the rest of the day preparing the bounty for our combined birthday party. We usually celebrate with a colourful summery lunch with friends and family, seated at an outside communal table. After lunch, Paul pulls some serious reds out of his cellar – and every 5 January I wish I had done the dishes the night before.

When we hit a 'big birthday' we still do the lunch but have a significant birthday celebration later in the month when friends and family are all back from their holidays. For my thirtieth birthday it was a brunch party: we set up buffet tables around two barbecues and, like musicians at a jam session, guests came in and out of chatter groups to cook their own French toast or whisk up another batch of Hollandaise Sauce for Eggs Benedict.

In those days I was a born-again Martha Stewart follower, so dessert was a sumptuous pie table served later in the afternoon. It featured Blackbottom Pie, which was the signature dessert on the dessert trolley at Marbles Restaurant, the restaurant I owned with my business partner, David Jordan, when I was in my twenties. My mother had made me an enormous square sponge cake filled with raspberries and whipped cream, and decorated with rosebuds and herbs from her garden in Waikanae, which became the birthday centrepiece.

When I turned forty I was desperate not to have a party, but as the day grew closer and I became more accepting, I invited guests to a 6.30 p.m. party. We served champagne with continuous fingerfood, and later in the evening served Barbecued Fish with Ginger, Soy and Coriander, and timbales of Coconut Rice from a small supper station. Guests ate very informally, sitting wherever they could perch.

For my fiftieth birthday I planned a blow-out with 200 guests. To fit in all the wine and food experiences I wanted to share with my friends and family, the party started at 3.00 p.m. The afternoon was antipasto time with wood-fired oven pizza, oysters on the half-shell, duck liver parfait and big glassfuls of pinot gris. At 5.30 p.m. we moved to another area of the garden for champagne with Chicken Tarragon Sandwiches. My aunt and uncle, Dorothy and Peter Moody, had given us some excellent advice in the early days of planning our garden at Springfield. They told us to plan our garden in rooms, so thanks to them our house is now surrounded by what seems like an extension of itself.

At 7.00 p.m. the party shifted to another outdoor room where a marquee was set up for a buffet dinner of crayfish and spit-roasted lamb. I was on such a high all night that I didn't eat anything, so was pleased to find serious leftovers in the fridge the next day. I talked to everybody at the party, and danced with as many men as possible. Later I saw photographs and heard stories from guests of how superb the food had been. The following Saturday I wished I could have had the party all over again.

Eugene Casey is an old friend of mine; in fact he worked for me as a sous chef in my restaurant days. He has spent the last fifteen years in London, returning most years to visit his family and friends. His fortieth birthday coincided with a trip home and I was delighted he accepted my offer to hold his party at Springfield. He was aware that many of the guests would not know each other, so we decided upon an informal party, similar to my fortieth. We began mid-afternoon, because it was a Sunday, so an early finish suited those guests who had to drive back to the city. Eugene wanted an early night too as he was flying home the following day.

Eugene and I spent an enthralling afternoon, the day before the party, making newspaper cones for the fish and chips, kneading dough for burger buns, gossiping and drinking Margaritas made with the tequila that was left over from the Tequila-lime Granita.

I surprised Eugene with his birthday cake – of sorts. I prepared the cakes a week before his arrival and had frozen them. He said he didn't want any fuss so I knew candles on a big cake were out of the question. Lettered cup-cakes were the answer and those guests who didn't want to compromise wine for cake were happy to take one home.

Our catering kitchen spends many hours making cocktail-sized food – we call it passarounds. When entertaining at home, do not be tempted to incorporate more than one or two passarounds into the menu as they are very time-consuming to prepare. Supplement passarounds with plattered rustic-style food, or food like my version of fish and chips in this chapter, which gives you more bang for your time.

Eugene and I spent an enthralling afternoon, the day before the party, making newspaper cones for the fish and chips, kneading dough for burger buns, gossiping and drinking Margaritas made with the tequila that was left over from the Tequila-lime Granita.

↑

Sue and Gary Walden from the Vege Nook

→

The roadside vegetable stall of Philip and Sue Sue

→ →

Zucchini and squash

→

Chilli Philly

Chilli Philly

Chilli Philly

SERVES 10–12 AS A PASSAROUND

250g Philadelphia cream
cheese

4 tblsp Tomato Chilli Jam
(see below)

2 tblsp chopped coriander

rice crackers

+ *This is the easiest dip in the world and once you start eating it, it is very difficult to stop.*

+ Place cream cheese on a platter, or in a shallow bowl. Dollop with Tomato Chilli Jam and sprinkle with coriander. Serve with rice crackers.

Tomato Chilli Jam

MAKES 400ML

500g (5-6) ripe tomatoes (cores
removed and roughly
chopped)

4 red chillies

10g (5) garlic cloves (peeled)

20g (2 thumbs) ginger (peeled
and roughly chopped)

30ml (2 tblsp) Thai fish sauce

300g (1 cup + ⅓ cup + 2 tblsp)
castor sugar

100ml (6 tblsp + 2 tsp) red
wine vinegar

+ *My friend Peter Gordon from Providores in London gave me this recipe, and I am lost if I don't have a jar of this in my larder. I use it on eggs, cheese, rice, fish, and chicken; you name it, Tomato Chilli Jam enhances it.*

+ Place half of the tomatoes, all of the chillies, garlic, ginger and fish sauce in a blender or a food processor and blend to a fine purée.

+ Place the purée, sugar and vinegar in a non-reactive pot and bring to the boil slowly, stirring all the time.

+ Cut remaining tomatoes into 5mm dice, including seeds.

+ Turn heat down to a medium boil and add diced tomatoes.

+ Cook on a medium boil for 20–25 minutes, stirring every 5 minutes to release the solids that settle on the bottom. Be sure to scrape the sides of the saucepan during cooking so the entire mass cooks evenly.

+ When it is ready, the jam will look thick and be fully amalgamated. If you wish, apply the standard jam test.

+ Pour into sterilised jars and seal. Tomato Chilli Jam can be kept for up to 12 months.

←

Parmesan-crumbed Fish
with Spicy Oven Wedges
in Newspaper Cones

Parmesan-crumbed Fish with Spicy Oven Wedges in Newspaper Cones

MAKES 20 COCKTAIL SERVES

Newspaper Cones

Parmesan-crumbed Fish
 (see page 54)

Spicy Oven Wedges
 (see page 55)

+ *These are always the most adored item at a party, particularly after a few drinks. Use a firm fish like hapuka, blue cod or orange roughy.*

+ Pile Parmesan-crumbed Fish and Spicy Oven Wedges into newspaper cones and serve hot immediately.

+ To make a newspaper cone, cut a sheet of newspaper into a square 28 x 28cm. Fold the square into a triangle and place the bottom of the triangle closest to you. Take the right-hand corner and pull it up to the top of the triangle. Wrap left-hand side of triangle around to centre back of triangle and then secure with a staple or sticky tape. Line the cone with greaseproof paper.

→

Parmesan-crumbed Fish
with Spicy Oven Wedges
in Newspaper Cones

Parmesan-crumbed Fish

MAKES 20 COCKTAIL SERVES

80g (1 cup) fresh breadcrumbs

20g (¼ cup) finely grated
  Parmesan cheese

½ tsp Maldon sea salt

¼ tsp freshly ground pepper

1 egg

30ml (2 tblsp) water

400g fresh fish (cut into 20g
  portions)

70g (½ cup) flour (lightly
  seasoned)

olive oil (for frying)

1 lemon (cut in half)

Maldon sea salt and freshly
  ground pepper

+ *Friends always tell me they hate fried food. We rarely serve
it when we cater, but at home I find, despite everyone's
protestations, it romps out. This fish is shallow-fried in olive
oil. When you have leftover bread or crusts, break into pieces,
process in a food processor until crumbed, then freeze for
next time you need fresh breadcrumbs.*

+ In a shallow container combine breadcrumbs, Parmesan, salt and pepper.

+ In a separate bowl place egg and water and whisk lightly to combine.

+ Dip fish portions into flour and gently shake to remove excess. Then dip
  fish into egg mixture, and into breadcrumbs.

+ Place in a single layer onto a tray lined with plastic wrap and refrigerate for
  about an hour before cooking. You could leave fish overnight if you wish.

+ Heat a heavy-based frypan and cover base with olive oil. When oil is hot
  (i.e. if it sizzles when you scatter a few breadcrumbs in it), place fish
  portions into pan and cook for 2–3 minutes on each side or until golden
  brown and fish is cooked through. Do not overcrowd the pan.

+ Using a fish slice remove fish from pan and drain on paper towels. To keep
  cooked fish warm as you continue to cook remaining fish portions, cover
  with a heavy tea towel.

+ Squeeze lemon juice over fish and then season before serving.
  Serve immediately.

Spicy Oven Wedges

MAKES 20 COCKTAIL SERVES

1–1.5kg (7) medium potatoes
(washed and dried)

45ml (3 tblsp) olive oil

1 tsp chicken stock powder

1 tsp paprika

1 tsp salt

½ tsp freshly ground black
pepper

Maldon sea salt and freshly
ground black pepper

+ *Agria or Desirée potatoes are superb for wedges. Avoid new
potatoes, and always make more than you think your guests
will eat.*

+ Preheat oven to 230°C.

+ Cut potatoes into thick wedges and place in a large roasting dish.
Toss with oil.

+ In a small bowl combine chicken stock powder, paprika, and salt and pepper.
Using a small sieve, sprinkle over the potatoes and toss to coat thoroughly.

+ Bake in oven 30–40 minutes until potatoes are cooked on the inside and
crispy on the outside. Test with a metal skewer or knife.

+ Drain on paper towels and season to taste.

BURGERS

Homemade burgers wow your guests because they will always taste better than what they buy. I like to serve baby burgers as a passaround, or large burgers later in the evening when guests are looking for something a little more substantial.

At home my burgers usually contain the beef mince patties, but I also like to serve lamb mince patties and include rocket and Tzatziki between the buns. Barbecued chicken thigh with bacon, tomato and avocado is another really worthy combination, and Parmesan-crumbed Fish prepared in 60g pieces between a bun with Tartare Sauce and shredded iceberg lettuce is an absolute winner.

It is difficult to purchase suitable burger buns. Firstly, there is the size issue: cocktail burger buns need to be not more than 3cm in diameter and very few bakeries will make this size. You need soft white bread with a small amount of chew, so that the buns do not become soggy sponges that fall apart as they are eaten.

Making your own buns is not necessarily a daunting task. I make them up to two weeks ahead and freeze them unbaked before the final rising.

For Eugene's party, we served large-sized Fillet of Beef Burgers later in the evening. I barbecued a whole fillet and we displayed all the fillings in bowls so guests could assemble their own burgers. Eugene's brother, a farmer from the Waikato, said it was the best burger he had ever eaten – and consumed three

Emma Vodanovich about to enjoy a
Fillet of Beef Burger with Béarnaise
Butter, Bacon, Lettuce and Tomato

MAKES 40 COCKTAIL-SIZED BURGERS
OR 10 LARGE BURGERS

40 cocktail-sized Burger Buns
    or 10 large Burger Buns
    (cut in half) (see opposite page)

Béarnaise Butter (see page 60)

1 lettuce (variety of your choice,
    but needs to be a soft lettuce)

8 tomatoes (each cut into 5 thick
    slices, discarding ends)

Maldon sea salt and freshly
    ground black pepper

olive oil (for cooking patties)

40 cocktail-sized Beef Burger
    Patties or 10 large Beef
    Burger Patties (see page 60)

300g (20 rashers) bacon

Beef Burgers

+   Spread cut sides of Burger Buns with Béarnaise Butter. Place a piece of
    lettuce on the bottom half of each bun, top with a slice of tomato, or for
    large burgers, with 4 slices, then season.

+   On a heated barbecue flat plate, or a heavy-based frypan, smear a little olive
    oil and cook Beef Burger Patties for 2–3 minutes on each side for cocktail
    size and 5–6 minutes for larger size, or until brown on each side and medium
    rare in the centre. Season patties.

+   Cook bacon on flat plate, or in frypan, until crispy and drain on paper towels.

+   Place Beef Burger Patties and bacon on top of tomato.

+   Top with the other half of burger buns and skewer with a small toothpick.
    I like to use toothpicks that come with paper flags attached to them.

Burger Buns

MAKES 40 COCKTAIL-SIZED BURGER BUNS OR 10 LARGE BURGER BUNS

8g (2 tsp) active dried yeast granules

15g (1 tblsp) sugar

125ml (½ cup) lukewarm water

50g butter (melted)

250ml (1 cup) milk

1½ tsp Maldon sea salt

490g (3½ cups) baker's flour (plus extra for dusting)

olive oil for greasing bowl

+ *Your supermarket may not stock flour identified as baker's flour. A baker also calls it strong flour as it is flour with a high gluten content. Gluten is the protein in flour that helps the strands of dough to rise. Your best alternative is high grade flour, which is suitable for heavier cakes and bread.*

+ Into a small bowl, place yeast, sugar and water. Combine briefly, then leave until frothy, approximately 5–15 minutes.

+ Combine butter, milk and salt in a jug, and warm to the same temperature as the yeast mixture. I do this in the microwave, or you could place jug in a bowl of hot water.

+ Place flour in the bowl of an electric mixer.

+ Add milk mixture and yeast and, using the dough hook, slowly mix until just combined and dough forms a ball. If a little flour remains on the bottom of the bowl, add a tablespoon more of cold water while mixer is running to incorporate that flour into the dough.

+ Transfer dough to a lightly oiled large bowl and cover bowl with plastic wrap. This creates a warm environment for the dough. Place bowl in a warm place until dough rises to twice its original size. It will take an hour at least to rise.

+ Turn dough out of bowl and knead until smooth and shiny. For cocktail-sized Burger Buns, break dough into 20g pieces and shape into little balls (40 balls). For large Burger Buns, break dough into 80g pieces and shape into balls (10 balls).

+ Spray 2 baking trays with oil and place balls on a tray, spacing approximately 1.5cm apart. This allows room for proving, but buns will also join together slightly which prevents them from drying out in the oven.

+ Cover loosely with oiled plastic wrap and place tray in a warm area. Prove for a further 30–45 minutes or until balls have doubled in size.

+ Using a sieve, dust with flour.

+ Preheat oven to 230°C.

+ Remove plastic wrap from tray and bake cocktail-sized Burger Buns for 10 minutes or large Burger Buns for 15 minutes, or until golden brown and cooked through.

+ Burger Buns can be made in advance and frozen raw. Once buns have been shaped (and before proving the second time), cover with oiled plastic wrap and place in freezer for up to two weeks. Before service, leave buns to defrost in a warm place. Then leave them to prove until doubled in size. Preheat oven to 230°C, dust buns with flour and bake for 15–20 minutes.

Beef Burger Patties

MAKES 40 COCKTAIL-SIZED BEEF BURGER PATTIES OR 10 LARGE BEEF BURGER PATTIES

800g ribeye beef (minced)

100g (1 small) onion (finely chopped)

30ml (2 tblsp) soy sauce

6–8 drops Tabasco

1 egg (gently whisked)

3 tblsp finely chopped Italian parsley

12g (1 tblsp) tomato paste

1 tsp Maldon sea salt

½ tsp freshly ground black pepper

+ *These are only as good as the meat you put in them. Ribeye beef is marbled with fat, which imparts a very tasty flavour to the patties.*

+ Place all ingredients in a large bowl and combine well – your hands are the best tools.

+ Form into 40 25g patties or 10 100g patties. Aim for the diameter of the burgers to match the diameter of the buns. Place patties on a tray lined with plastic wrap.

+ Rest in refrigerator for at least 30 minutes before cooking. You can prepare these up to two days in advance; store with plastic wrap between each layer.

Béarnaise Butter

FOR 40 COCKTAIL-SIZED BEEF BURGERS OR 10 LARGE BEEF BURGERS

400g unsalted butter (chopped and softened)

1 tsp tarragon vinegar

2 tblsp lemon juice

bunch of fresh tarragon

Maldon sea salt and freshly ground pepper

+ *Tarragon grows well in our garden, and at the end of summer Clare Douglas, our gardener, cuts it right back. With this supply I dry some, but mostly I incorporate it into Béarnaise Butter and freeze to use later. I like Béarnaise Butter spread on crostini or sliced French bread with rare roasted beef, or as a herb butter with steak or mussels, and in winter I make Béarnaise Sauce from Béarnaise Butter.*

+ Place butter, vinegar and lemon juice into a food processor fitted with a metal blade and process until smooth.

+ Strip tarragon leaves off stalks, discard stalks, and finely chop leaves.

+ Add tarragon to butter mixture and combine briefly using the pulse button on food processor. Do not over-process as butter will go green.

+ Add seasoning to taste.

Fillet of Beef Burgers with Béarnaise Butter, Bacon, Lettuce and Tomato

MAKES 10 LARGE BURGERS

1.2kg beef fillet

125ml (½ cup) olive oil

freshly ground black pepper

rosemary and bay leaf sprigs

300g (20 rashers) bacon

10 Large Burger Buns
   (see page 59)

Béarnaise Butter
   (see opposite page)

1 lettuce (variety of your choice,
   but it needs to be a soft
   lettuce)

8 tomatoes (each cut into 5cm
   thick slices, discarding ends)

Maldon sea salt and freshly
   ground black pepper

+ *This is the most luxurious of beef burgers, but the easiest to prepare. You can use prepared horseradish in place of Béarnaise Butter if you prefer.*

+ Trim beef fillet of silverskin and fat, and remove the chain. Your butcher can do this for you.

+ Drizzle olive oil over beef, add pepper and toss beef to give an even coating of oil. Place in a bowl with herbs and refrigerate for at least 1 hour but preferably overnight.

+ 1 hour before cooking take beef out of refrigerator.

+ Preheat barbecue to high, or preheat an oven to 220°C.

+ If barbecuing, sear beef on all sides on barbecue flat plate or grill plate and cook for 10–12 minutes on each side, or until cooked medium-rare. Remove beef from barbecue, place in a roasting tray, cover tray with a heavy tea towel and rest for 10–15 minutes away from heat.

+ If cooking in oven, place on a low-sided roasting tray and cook for 15–20 minutes, or until cooked medium-rare. Remove beef from oven, cover roasting tray with a heavy tea towel and rest beef for 10–15 minutes away from heat.

+ While beef is resting, cook bacon on barbecue, or spread out on a low-sided baking tray and cook at the same oven temperature as beef for 5–10 minutes, or until crispy.

+ Drain bacon on paper towels.

+ Split Burger Buns horizontally through the centre and spread cut sides with Béarnaise Butter. Place bacon, lettuce and tomato on bottom halves and season.

+ Slice fillet into 5–8mm thick slices, place a slice on bottom bun half and season. Top with bun half and if you wish secure with a skewer or toothpick.

Clark's Dress-Me-Up or Just-Eat-Me Chocolate Cup-cakes

+ *Julie Clark, owner of the iconic Clark's Café in the Wellington Public Library and a wholesale bakery called Cake, gave me this recipe, but as a single big cake. It is the most versatile chocolate cake recipe I have ever owned. Here I have adapted it to cup-cakes, which I make regularly and serve in many guises. In fact, I always have some in the freezer iced and ready to go. This is the 'dress-me-up' version.*

MAKES 18 MUFFIN-SIZED CUP-CAKES

100g (½ cup + 1 tblsp) dark chocolate buttons (or slab chopped into pieces)

175g (¾ cup + 2 tblsp) brown sugar

375ml (1½ cups) milk (heated to almost boiling)

125g butter (chopped and softened)

220g (1 cup + 2 tblsp) brown sugar

2 eggs (lightly beaten)

250g (1½ cups + 6 tblsp) plain flour

30g (¼ cup) cocoa

5g (1 tsp) baking soda

Ganache (see below)

+ Preheat oven to 180°C. Line 18 muffin tins with 18 paper cases. The mixture is very runny, so it is important to place paper cases in muffin tins so that the cup-cakes are supported.

+ In a heavy-based saucepan place chocolate, first measure of brown sugar and milk. Stir over a low heat until chocolate is melted. The mixture will appear curdled. Set aside.

+ Using an electric mixer or a wooden spoon, cream butter and second measure of brown sugar until mixture looks pale and creamy.

+ Add eggs to the butter mixture, combining well.

+ Sift flour, cocoa and baking soda together and add to butter mixture. Combine well, then add chocolate mixture and stir.

+ Pour mixture into paper cases. Bake for 20–25 minutes or until cup-cakes spring back when gently prodded.

+ Remove from oven and, when cool enough to touch, remove cup-cakes in paper cases from muffin tins.

+ When cold, ice with Ganache. Leave in a cool place for Ganache to set, but not in the fridge. Decorate with a piped message.

+ Store cup-cakes at room temperature or in the freezer.

Ganache

MAKES 300ML

175ml (½ cup + 3 tblsp + 1 tsp) cream

175g dark chocolate (buttons or slab chopped into pieces)

+ Pour the cream into a medium-sized saucepan and place over a medium heat. Bring to just below boiling point, then remove from heat and add chocolate. Stir until chocolate is melted and the sauce is smooth.

+ Leave to cool completely, out of the fridge, and apply when it begins to go tacky.

→

Clark's Dress-Me-Up or Just-Eat-Me
Chocolate Cup-cakes made into a
birthday cake for Eugene

How to Decorate Your Cup-cakes

MAKES 120ML

75g (½ cup) white chocolate
(buttons or slab chopped
into pieces) (melted)

+ Fit your piping bag with a size 2 or 3 (small) nozzle.

+ Pour melted chocolate into piping bag.

+ Place piping bag between your thumb and forefinger and push the filling down towards the nozzle, at the same time removing any air pockets that have formed. Twist the bag so it is closed at the top.

+ Hold the bag by resting the twisted end between your thumb and fingers. Apply pressure to the top of the bag only, using the palm of your hand. Use the other hand to guide the tip.

+ Before you begin piping, squeeze out some of the filling into a bowl to make sure there are no air pockets.

+ Point the tip down onto the cup-cake and apply pressure as you pipe and release the pressure when you want to stop. Piping in one swift movement is easier than a slow stopping and starting.

+ Decorate with a message, name, letters, numbers or a shape.

→

Tequila-lime Granita

Tequila-lime Granita

Tequila-lime Granita

MAKES 600ML/10 SHOOTER GLASSES

100g (½ cup) sugar

250ml (1 cup) water

62.5ml (¼ cup) liquid glucose

187.5ml (¾ cup) white tequila

125ml (½ cup) freshly
    squeezed lime juice

62.5ml (¼ cup) Triple Sec

+ *A refreshing end to a party. If you wish, before guests arrive, fill the shooter glasses and place back in freezer until you are ready to serve.*

+ Make a syrup by placing sugar and water in a pot and, over a medium heat, stirring until sugar dissolves. Increase heat and boil until small bubbles appear evenly across the surface of the syrup. Add glucose and stir until combined, then cool. (Liquid glucose adds sweetness to the granita without adding extra sugar, which would hinder the freezing. It is available at some chemists or at our shop.)

+ In a small saucepan, bring tequila to a boil and reduce by half (the flavour will be intensified and the alcohol will be burnt off). Cool.

+ Combine tequila with syrup, lime juice and Triple Sec.

+ Pour mixture into a shallow container and freeze. As it freezes (it will take 6–8 hours or overnight), 3 or 4 times during the freezing break up ice crystals with a fork.

+ Fork into shooter glasses to serve.

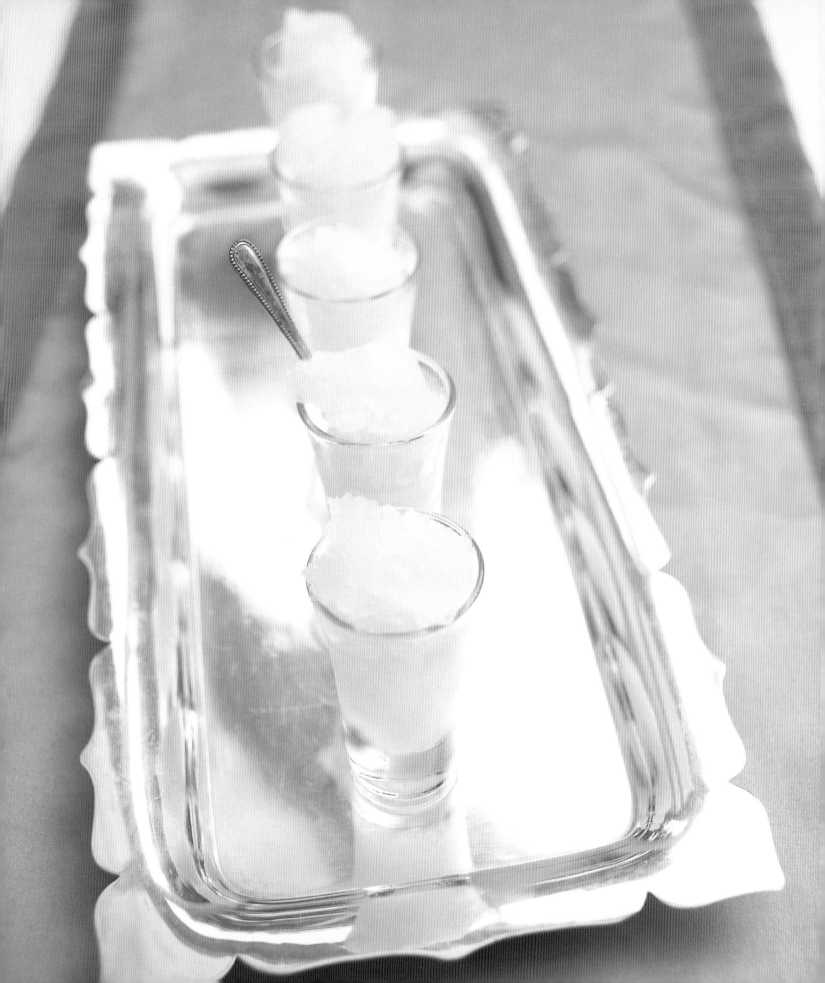

A WOOD-FIRED OVEN

I am a magazine fiend and feel deprived if I don't read at least ten a month – they have to be food, wine or lifestyle. One evening I was reading an article comparing different styles of wood-fired ovens and cooks' preferences, and happened to mention to Paul that a wood-fired oven would add a new dimension to our entertaining. I went on to say that it would be a selling point for the small 'hands on' cooking classes I take at the house, and then carried on reading. Very soon I began to rue the day I had mentioned wood-fired ovens. I had never said I actually wanted one, but I had a feeling one was about to appear.

Several days later a book arrived via Amazon.com called *The Bread Builders: Hearth Loaves and Masonry Ovens*. I thought it must be a mistake because I am the one who orders the cookbooks and I certainly hadn't ordered this one. Shortly afterwards the brickie showed up and went into a private consultation with Paul. They went outside to our barbecue area and began to do the man thing of stepping out measurements. The brickie duly departed with the new book, plus little 'post-its' flapping from some pages and his border collie yelping from the truck tray.

A few days later I was shopping when a woman came up to me announcing that we had a brickie in common and when my wood-fired oven was complete could she come and see it. I think I frightened her with my stunned look.

Lo and behold, two weeks later, with still no discussion between Paul and me on the subject, the brickie and his team arrived. Stakes went into the ground, with string tied between, and digging began. The foundations were built, and wheelbarrow after wheelbarrow of local stones began to appear. Before I could say ciabatta, we had a wood-fired oven. Paul's only comment to me was that now I had one I had better learn how to use it.

For a few weeks I just looked at it, trying to gather the time and energy to read the artisan version of a how-to-do manual on ovens. A visitor asked me if I was planning to sell my pottery, believing that this oven, for the cook who has everything, was a kiln.

With trial and error I slowly learned the ways of the fire. If you have ever grown heirloom tomatoes, you will understand the complexity of mastering a wood–fired oven. The end result is outstanding, but the troublesome process of reaching closure illustrates very clearly why wood-fired ovens and heirloom tomatoes have been superseded. Heirloom tomatoes are prone to every fungicide and pest that God ever conceived for a vegetable garden. Their care and nurturing becomes a life mission. This is how it is for a wood-fired oven.

Firstly, take your wood, the correct wood not any old wood, and chop it to fit your oven. Friends began to send me pictures of cooks in national dress from a myriad countries tending their wood-fired ovens with depressed ravenous visages, the insinuation being that I was having problems because I was wearing the wrong clothes.

The oven devours wood – and only likes hardwood. But our area only produces softwood, so the wood for our oven has to travel a minimum of one hour. It then has to be chopped to fit the oven, and the oven lit at least five hours before you commence cooking. Considering this preparation, it seems absurd that a pizza cooks in the oven in under five minutes. However, you do begin to think it is all worthwhile when you eat the pizza, with crisp base like you have never experienced before and the delicious smoky flavoured toppings.

But the most amazing thing about the oven is that at the end of each pizza cook-up we can place lunch in the oven for the following day. It might be a pork shoulder coated in fennel seeds, which is slow-cooked for hours until it is meltingly tender and aromatic, or a leg of lamb studded with garlic. It is left in overnight, and one wakes up joyful knowing that a midday repast is nearly ready.

There is another bonus to owning a wood-fired oven – working with children.

I have never had children of my own so for years I have felt like a benevolent grandmother. I really enjoy children and coerce them into helping me as much as possible. I get them to choose place-mats and napkins, pick and arrange table flowers and set the table. They are usually dedicated to the job and really keen to learn the finer points. Parents joke that I am recruiting them for our catering company. Kids can peel, sometimes chop, definitely stir and, if told the safety issues simply enough, become great barbecuers, and even better pizza-makers.

I have fond memories as a child of going to hotels for dinner with my family and being treated as a guest rather than a child. It was marvellous to order from an adult menu and have waiters call you 'madam'. I don't think special children's menus existed in those days.

I used to love helping my mother, who always encouraged me to help her cook. I would stand on a stool to make gravy and squash the flour lumps out with a fish slice. I had full command of a Kenwood by the time I was eight and afghans were a speciality. My domain was iceberg salad with grated cheese, carrot and Highlander condensed milk dressing, and my flummery sat proud in coloured wine glasses.

On this particular occasion I invited our friends Julie and Lloyd with their five children, and Murray, my photographer, with his son Oscar, to lunch. Fortunately Murray remembered to bring his camera. And it was this day that I discovered a real bonus to owning a wood-fired oven: it eliminates the need for a swimming pool as it is entertainment for everyone. I found that the adults and kids loved to help with the fire and even begged to make pizza. Pizza dough takes time to rise and this was an enormous advantage. While the yeast was doing its thing, the kids rode their bikes, caught an eel and continued to disturb our hens in the hope of one more egg. There is always a sense of anticipation with dough, and the children came back and forth to check its progress. The best part of all though was the kneading. I divided the dough up so that all the children had a ball and convinced myself that after it was thrown, and dropped, it is perfectly hygienic to pick the grass off and proceed.

I put all the toppings out and let the kids construct their own pizzas. With the thought of future staff members in mind, I gave little pads to the children so they could take pizza orders from the adults.

I am giving you the recipe for Elliot Morrison's topping, which he feels will appeal greatly to seven-year-olds and also my order for toppings that I placed with Maddie Morrison on the day.

I am continuing with my wood-fired oven research and, who knows, before long Springfield may be available for dial-up pizzas.

For a few weeks I just looked at it trying to gather the time and energy to read the artisan version of a how-to-do manual on ovens. A visitor asked me if I was planning to sell my pottery, believing that this oven, for the cook who has everything, was a kiln.

← Homemade pizza with a crispy base and simple toppings cooked in a wood-fired oven tastes better than any pizza you have ever experienced

Elliot's Wood-fired Oven Pizza

MAKES ONE 28CM PIZZA

250ml (1cup) Springfield
 Tomato Sauce
 (see opposite page)

1 28cm pizza base
 (see page 72)

150g (1–2) sausages (cut
 thinly on the diagonal)

100g (6 rashers) bacon
 (roughly chopped)

120g (1 cup) grated
 tasty cheese

30g (6 tblsp) Parmesan
 cheese (finely grated)

+ *This was Elliot's choice of toppings when he came for lunch.*
 He says children will enjoy making it provided they are allowed
 to grate their own Parmesan on a microplane™ as he was.

+ Spread Springfield Tomato Sauce on pizza base.

+ Layer sausage slices on top and sprinkle with bacon.

+ Sprinkle with tasty cheese and top with Parmesan.

+ Bake in a very hot wood-fired oven for 3–5 minutes, or bake in a 220°C
 oven for 15–20 minutes, or until base is crisp and lightly coloured.

Ruth's Wood-fired Oven Pizza

MAKES ONE 28CM PIZZA

250ml (1cup) Springfield Tomato
 Sauce (see opposite page)

1 28cm pizza base (see page 72)

10–12 basil leaves (ripped roughly)

35g (4–5 slices) prosciutto (each
 slice cut in 3 lengthwise)

60g (16–20) black olives
 (stoned and sliced)

30g (6 tblsp) Parmesan cheese
 (finely grated)

+ *A pizza with a thin crispy base requires a minimalist approach to*
 the topping. The choices are limitless, but when someone takes
 my order this is my favourite combination.

+ Spread Springfield Tomato Sauce on pizza base.

+ Sprinkle sauce with basil. Lay prosciutto evenly over basil and
 sprinkle with olives.

+ Top with Parmesan.

+ Bake in a very hot wood-fired oven for 3–5 minutes or bake at 220°C
 for 15–20 minutes, or until base is crispy and lightly coloured.

→
Springfield Tomato Sauce on stove-top in my
stainless-steel (non-reactive) preserving pan

Springfield Tomato Sauce

MAKES 750ML

2kg (14–18) ripe tomatoes

10g (2 tsp) butter

10ml (2 tsp) olive oil

20g (2) shallots (finely
    chopped)

2 garlic cloves (finely chopped)

1 fresh red chilli (deseeded and
    finely chopped)

2 fresh bay leaves

Maldon sea salt and freshly
    ground black pepper

+   *This isn't a preserve – it is a fresh sauce. With tomatoes from Sue
    Sue, a local and extraordinary grower, I often make pots of this
    sauce and freeze it to use in winter to toss through pasta, to cover
    a pizza base or as a foundation for a sauce to go with meat. In
    summer I always like to have it on hand in the fridge.*

+   To remove skin from tomatoes, cut a cross on base of tomatoes and then
    place in a large bowl. Cover tomatoes with boiling water and leave to sit
    for a few minutes, or until the skin begins to peel away.

+   Remove tomatoes from the water, spread out and when cool enough
    to handle peel skin away from flesh. Cut out the core, cut tomatoes
    in half width-ways and deseed. Discard seeds and juice.

+   Finely chop tomato flesh.

+   Place a medium to large non-reactive saucepan over a medium heat,
    add butter and oil and melt butter.

+   Add shallots, garlic and chilli, and sauté for 2–3 minutes or until soft.
    Do not brown.

+   Add tomatoes, bay leaves, 1 tsp salt and bring to the boil. Turn heat down
    and simmer for 50–60 minutes or until sauce is thick and 'saucy'.

+   Remove bay leaves and season to taste.

→

Ruth's Wood-fired
Oven Pizza

Pizza Dough

MAKES 3 28CM BASES

10g (1 tblsp) castor sugar

6g (2 tsp) dried yeast

215ml (¾ cup + 1 tblsp +
2 tsp) warm water

450g (3 cups + 4 tblsp)
high grade flour

½ tsp salt

45ml (3 tblsp) olive oil

a little extra olive oil

+ *I like to make this dough with baker's flour, which unfortunately isn't usually available in supermarkets. High grade flour is a suitable replacement though.*

+ Combine sugar and yeast in a small bowl with 90ml of the water and set aside in a warm place for 5 minutes until it foams.

+ Place flour and salt in a large bowl. Make a well in centre of flour and pour in olive oil, remaining 125mls water and yeast mixture.

+ Move the water from well outwards mixing to incorporate flour. Mix until the dough comes together. You may need to add a little more water. The dough should be soft but dry to the touch.

+ Transfer dough to a lightly floured surface and knead for at least 8 minutes or until it feels smooth and supple.

+ Place a little oil in a large bowl and rub it around the inside surface. Place dough in the bowl and roll it until it is coated in oil. Cover bowl with a tea towel (or plastic wrap if you want quicker action) and leave in a warm place until double in volume, about 45 minutes–1¼ hours. Alternatively, the dough can be placed in the refrigerator to rise slowly. This will take approximately 8 hours.

+ Punch the dough down to its original size and divide into 3 portions. At this stage the dough can be stored in the refrigerator for 4 hours or frozen. Bring the dough back to room temperature before continuing.

+ Take one portion of dough and roll out to a 28cm circle. Repeat with the remaining dough.

+ Transfer the dough to a lightly floured tray and proceed with toppings.

→
Sausage Rolls made
for the children

Sausage Rolls

MAKES 14 LUNCH-SIZED ROLLS

15ml (1 tblsp) olive oil

50g (¼) onion (finely chopped)

500g pork sausage meat

30ml (2 tblsp) Springfield
Tomato Sauce (see page
71) (or a commercial bottled
or tinned tomato sauce)

2 tblsp finely chopped Italian
parsley

2–3 drops Tabasco sauce

½ tsp Maldon sea salt

¾ tsp freshly ground black
pepper

400g (2½ sheets pre-rolled)
puff pastry (defrosted)

egg glaze made with 1 egg
yolk and 1 tblsp water,
lightly beaten

+ *I don't cook special meals for kids, but I do like to include dishes that they find really tasty. Their parents also usually adore old-fashioned sausage rolls like these. I use pure pork sausage meat purchased from our local butcher.*

+ Place a small frypan on stove top over a medium heat. When hot, smear frypan with olive oil, add onion and cook without browning until soft. Cool.

+ Place sausage meat, tomato sauce, parsley, Tabasco, and salt and pepper in a bowl, add onion and mix thoroughly.

+ Lay pastry sheets out on a lightly floured bench and cut 2 whole sheets into halves. You will now have 5 rectangles of pastry.

+ Divide the sausage meat mixture into five.

+ Using cold wet hands, place one portion of sausage mixture along the long edge of a pastry rectangle in a thick sausage shape about 3cm in diameter. Repeat for the other four pastry rectangles.

+ Roll up to enclose sausage meat in pastry, moistening one edge to ensure pastry edges stick together.

+ Preheat oven to 210°C.

+ Cut rolls into even pieces 7– 8cm long and place on greased oven trays. Rest in refrigerator for 30 minutes.

+ Remove from refrigerator and brush with egg glaze.

+ Bake for 15–20 minutes until golden brown. Serve immediately, or cool and reheat before serving. Accompany with your favourite chutney.

Vita Morrison, whose favourite colour
is pink, enjoying a Raspberry Fizzy

Raspberry Fizzy

MAKES 6 TALL GLASSES

190g (1½ cups) fresh
   raspberries

35g (3 tblsp + 1 tsp) castor
   sugar

ice

1 litre (4 cups) water

lemonade (well chilled)

1 lemon (thinly sliced)

6 mint leaves

+ *Kids adore this brightly coloured fizzy drink. Try it yourself on a hot
day with a muddled lime and a shot of vodka.*

+ Into a food processor fitted with a plastic blade place raspberries and sugar.
Process until fruit is smooth, but not until the seeds are crushed as this
would make the drink bitter.

+ To remove seeds from raspberry purée, strain purée through a fine sieve.
Use a ladle to push purée through. Discard seeds.

+ Transfer purée to a covered container and keep chilled until ready to make
Raspberry Fizzy.

+ Half fill a long glass with ice. Pour 2 tblsp raspberry purée on ice and top up
with lemonade. Stir to combine and finish with a slice of lemon and a mint
leaf. Serve immediately.

→

Oscar Lloyd eating an Orange Jelly

Orange Jelly

+ *Many children have only tasted packet jelly so fresh fruit jellies are a whole new ball game. The purple heartsease, which is a tiny pansy, look really pretty set in the jelly.*

MAKES 600ML, SERVES 6

45ml (3 tblsp) water

11g (1 tblsp + 1 tsp) gelatine

500ml (2 cups) freshly squeezed orange juice

150g (¾ cup) sugar

3 oranges (cut in half with the pulp scooped out to form cups)

12 heartsease (pansies)

+ Place water in a small bowl. Soften gelatine by sprinkling over water and leaving to sit for 10 minutes or until gelatine has absorbed the water.

+ Pour orange juice into a medium-sized, non-reactive pot and add sugar. Over a medium heat stir with a metal spoon until sugar is dissolved. Bring to the boil then remove from heat. Add softened gelatine and stir until dissolved. Cool.

+ Strain syrup to remove any orange pith or gelatine strands and pour into orange cups. Leave to set in refrigerator 30–45 minutes, or until just starting to set.

+ Place two heartsease into each jelly and gently push beneath the surface.

+ Place back in refrigerator to set firmly.

+ Serve with or without Vanilla Bean Ice-cream (see page 183).

→

Marinated Chicken Nibbles and
Garlic Sour Cream Dipping Sauce
with Spicy Oven Wedges

Marinated Chicken Nibbles

SERVES 6–8

45ml (3 tblsp) Tamari soy
sauce

15ml (1 tblsp) honey

15ml (1 tblsp) olive oil

freshly ground black pepper

1 garlic clove (finely chopped)

1kg (24) chicken nibbles

+ *I always cook bone-in chicken in the oven rather than on the barbecue. Chicken is brilliant barbecued, but impossible to successfully barbecue through to the bone.*

+ In a small bowl combine soy sauce, honey, oil, pepper and garlic to make the marinade.

+ Add chicken to the marinade and toss well to coat all pieces. Cover with plastic wrap and leave to marinate for 2–3 hours, or overnight, in the refrigerator.

+ Preheat oven to 190°C.

+ Remove chicken from the marinade and spread out on a low-sided baking tray.

+ Cook for 20–25 minutes or until the juices run clear when pierced with a knife.

+ Serve hot or cold.

Garlic Sour Cream Dipping Sauce for Spicy Oven Wedges

MAKES 250ML

85g (⅓ cup + 1 tblsp) cream
cheese (softened)

160g (⅔ cup) sour cream

1 garlic clove (crushed)

1 tsp honey

Maldon sea salt and freshly
ground black pepper

Spicy Oven Wedges
(see page 55)

+ *You can add herbs like chervil, chives or Dijon mustard to this dip, but kids usually enjoy it best without the hint of green.*

+ Place cream cheese and sour cream into a bowl and combine until mixture is smooth.

+ Add garlic and honey and combine. Season to taste.

+ Serve in a small bowl as a dipping sauce with Spicy Oven Wedges.

←
Meringues with
Passionfruit Honey and
Whipped Cream

Meringues with Passionfruit Honey and Whipped Cream

MAKES 95–100 SMALL MERINGUES

4 (½ cup) egg whites

280g (1⅓ cups) castor sugar

pinch salt

Passionfruit Honey (see below)

Whipped Cream (see page 107)

+ *During the holidays I always have meringues in the pantry as they are an instant and adored dessert. Passionfruit Honey gives you that slightly offbeat sour taste, which is so delicious with something as sweet as meringues.*

+ Preheat oven to 120°C. Line 2 or 3 baking trays with baking paper.

+ Using an electric mixer, whisk egg whites for 20 seconds or until stiff peaks form.

+ With mixer still whisking, slowly pour in castor sugar and pinch salt.

+ When mixture is stiff and sugar is dissolved, dollop 3–4cm rounds on baking trays or pipe with a fluted nozzle.

+ Bake 45–50 minutes until meringues are crisp and dry throughout.

+ Cool completely and store in an airtight container in a cool place. They keep well for 2–3 weeks.

+ Serve with accompanying bowls of Passionfruit Honey and Whipped Cream.

Passionfruit Honey

MAKES 2¼ CUPS OR 562.5ML

1 egg yolk

3 eggs

220g (1 cup) sugar

50g butter (cut into very small dice)

190ml (¾ cup) passionfruit juice (obtained by straining passionfruit pulp)

+ *I freeze passionfruit pulp in autumn to have on hand for desserts as it is one of my favourite flavours. Making Passionfruit Honey in the microwave is far less troublesome than in a bain marie over a stove-top. Passionfruit Honey can be kept in the fridge for up to 1 month.*

+ Place egg yolk, eggs and sugar in a microwave-proof bowl and whisk until combined.

+ Add butter and passionfruit juice and whisk briefly. Place bowl in microwave and cook on high for 3–5 minutes, whisking after every minute, until the mixture is smooth, creamy and holds the mark of a whisk. (The whisking after every minute is crucial in this recipe.)

+ Cool for a few minutes then pour into sterilised jars and seal. Store in the refrigerator.

CHAMPAGNE INTERLUDES

A few years ago I was asked to cook a New Zealand dinner at Veuve Clicquot in Rheims, France, at the Widow Clicquot's mansion. The widow is, of course, long gone, but her home lives on in absolute glory and is used for hospitality by the champagne house she began. Paul and I decided it was an opportunity of a lifetime and planned the menu around the logistics of getting New Zealand produce to Rheims months ahead. It seemed a simple exercise compared to the restaurant we had manned three times, for a week at a time, at Anuga, the biggest food fair in the world, held in Cologne biannually.

Shelley Templer, our friend and colleague, was living in Belgium. Shelley had worked at Ruth Pretty Catering for many years and some time ago left to take up a job as chef at the New Zealand Embassy in Brussels. Since then she has married Rob and now runs her own successful catering business and cooking school, called Kauri Catering, in Brussels. We collected Shelley and our New Zealand produce in Brussels and drove to Rheims with a bootful of cervena, whitebait, lamb, koura, kiwifruit, honey and a supply of just-released Cloudy Bay sauvignon blanc.

It seemed like murder when the time came to prepare the koura for dinner. When we were kids we caught them in a very cold stream that runs through Karori Park, and we always threw them back. In Rheims they literally jumped out of their poly bin as though they were pleased to see us, exactly seventy-two hours since they had been plucked out of the mud at the bottom of a wintry pond in Alexandra.

After a fretful sleep in one of Madame's four-poster beds, I met Shelley in the kitchen at 6.00 a.m. to commence our duties. Dawn was just breaking as we pushed open the wooden shutters to reveal a perfect French garden, featuring topiary versions of Madame's favourite tree, the clementine mandarin. She named her daughter after the tree, and it later became the signature colour of the champagne house. The kitchen floor was made of flagstone, and uneven, and in the centre of the kitchen there was a large, battered, pine table where we placed our lists, notes and knives, ready for action.

Like mice just before humans wake up, we scuttled around the ground floor of the mansion spotting the impressively large D-end dining table overhung by a crystal chandelier of mighty proportions. We discovered consecutive sitting rooms, and were practising sitting on the sofas in our chef uniforms when we were interrupted by the maid arriving to offer us breakfast. It was very simple – warm baguettes with paste-like apricot jam and unsalted butter, coffee with warm milk and orange juice squeezed by the maid's fair hand.

I need no excuse to drink champagne; it suits every mood and all times of the day. It can be used for celebration or commiseration, and responds sterlingly to sharp, tantalising food tastes. It befits breakfast, lunch or dinner, or any meal in between.

That day we chopped, stirred and cooked as if in a dream. Reality finally snapped around 10.45 p.m. when dessert was served, dinner was over and the day had come to an end. We were led into the dining room and received a standing ovation and an invitation to return at any time.

Luckily for Paul, he was able to be a guest at the dinner and said he prayed for us and the waiters as they carried in the West Coast whitebait dish. The whitebait was sautéed in butter with garlic and lemon, and sat in a mound surrounded by a teepee made of asparagus spears – the teepees definitely required a steady hand.

The next day, Count Edouard de Nazelle, a descendant of Madame Clicquot, arranged a day in the country for the three of us, taking us in his Bentley to watch a pressing of grapes for Grande Dame, then onwards to Le Manoir de Verzy, set in a vineyard, a house which in previous times had been inhabited by the vineyard manager. The house has been magnificently restored, and plans were shown to us detailing the future restoration of a large glasshouse in the garden for artists in residence.

There were fifteen guests at the lunch in the country, and before we sat down Count Edouard made a surprise announcement with much pomp and ceremony. He inducted Paul and me into the Circle of Friends of the Widow and it was his pleasure to present us with the medals and documentation. There are 300 friends worldwide, and now, every year on our birthdays, we receive a bottle of Grande Dame each, accompanied by a personal card from Edouard. As Paul and I share a birthday, we drink one bottle on the day and save the other for celebrations to come.

I need no excuse to drink champagne; it suits every mood and all times of the day. It can be used for celebration or commiseration, and responds sterlingly to sharp, tantalising food tastes. It befits breakfast, lunch or dinner, or any meal in between. For a champagne interlude, aim for quality of food, not quantity. A champagne interlude can be enjoyed with one other person, with a group or even by yourself. I love to sit by myself in favourite places in my house and garden with a new magazine, or a foreign film on video, a long-distance extended phone call, or a beguiling book, with a glass or two of champagne. It's sheer luxury.

And if a friend pops in, it seems easier somehow to offer champagne rather than coffee, and I can always rustle up something simple but complementary, like grilled Gruyère on toast.

Sometimes I invite guests a little earlier than usual for dinner and begin proceedings in a part of the house or garden they wouldn't normally see. I serve a glass of champagne with delectable sandwiches like Chicken and Tarragon, or go all out with a Crayfish Sandwich. For fun sometimes I may include an *amuse-gueule* (a tiny offering) before the entrée, and serve a glass of champagne matched to a delicate morsel such as the very special cocktail-sized paua you can buy in New Zealand.

There's nothing quite like a champagne party. I find it a brilliant opportunity to invite a whole range of people because after one glass of bubbly guests seem to become particularly amiable and affable. I do make a point, however, of suggesting a finish time on the invitation because if nothing is planned afterwards, particularly in the way of food, one or two tired and emotional guests will want the party to go on all night.

 A bottle trolley used in French cellars holds empties

An interlude for two in the summer
house with champagne and
Chicken and Tarragon Sandwiches

Chicken and Tarragon Sandwiches

MAKES 24 COCKTAIL-SIZED SANDWICHES

6 black peppercorns

1 bay leaf

2 sprigs thyme

390g (1 double) chicken breast
(skin on) or 240g leftover
chicken

500ml (2 cups) milk

150g (½ cup + 4 tblsp) Basic
Mayonnaise (see page 189)

1½ tblsp chopped fresh French
tarragon leaves

½ tsp Maldon sea salt

¼ tsp freshly ground black pepper

12 slices white sandwich bread

butter for buttering bread

+ *A chicken sandwich is the perfect accompaniment for champagne
any time of the day. Tarragon grows extremely well in our garden
so I use it liberally in scrambled eggs, dressings and, in particular,
with chicken. In winter I sometimes use chervil instead of tarragon.*

+ Preheat oven to 200°C.

+ Place peppercorns, bayleaf, thyme and chicken into a roasting tray. Pour
milk over chicken and bake in oven for 30–40 minutes or until cooked.

+ Remove from oven, discard liquid and leave to cool.

+ When chicken is cold, remove skin and discard. Finely chop chicken
and place in a bowl with mayonnaise, tarragon, salt and pepper.

+ Spread each bread slice with butter and spread an even layer of
chicken mixture on 6 of the slices of bread.

+ Top with the other half of the slices to make sandwiches. Trim off
the crusts and cut into four triangles.

+ Store sandwiches in a sealed container in the fridge with paper
on the bottom of the container and between each layer.

Crayfish Sandwiches

MAKES 30 COCKTAIL SERVES

430g (1) crayfish tail (cooked)

15 slices thin white sandwich bread

30g (3 tblsp) butter (softened)

60ml (4 tblsp) Lemon Mayonnaise (see page 189)

4 tblsp finely chopped parsley

Maldon sea salt and freshly ground black pepper

+ *When I make crayfish sandwiches, I cut the bread before I put the filling in as I don't want to waste any of the precious meat. It is possible to make these sandwiches the day ahead if you refrigerate them in a plastic container with a tight-filling lid. It is very important to place wax paper between each layer and on the bottom of the container. To achieve 430g crayfish tail you need to begin with a live crayfish weighing about 1kg. To prepare a live crayfish, see page 98.*

+ Remove shell and intestinal tract from crayfish tail and slice crayfish meat into 5–7mm medallions. Set aside.

+ Using a 4.5cm round, straight-edge cutter, cut out 60 rounds of bread.

+ Butter each round and top with Lemon Mayonnaise.

+ Dip mayonnaise side of half the bread rounds in parsley and use these as sandwich bottoms.

+ Place a crayfish medallion on the parsley and season with salt and pepper.

+ Top the sandwich with the second bread round and serve immediately.

Panfried Paua with
Lemon

Panfried Paua with Lemon

MAKES 12 COCKTAIL SERVES

12 cocktail-sized paua (live
    and in their shells)

clarified butter

lemon juice

Maldon sea salt and freshly
    ground black pepper

+ *Your fish supplier can order this New Zealand delicacy for you. Tiny paua are for very special occasions and their delicate flavour is wonderful with champagne. Cocktail-sized paua are, of course, farmed and perfectly legal.*

+ To remove paua from the shell, hold shell upside-down and, starting at the narrow end of the shell, use your thumb to push against the shell, under the paua muscle, to cleanly remove paua.

+ Remove stomach sack from paua by pulling away from paua muscle. Discard stomach sack.

+ With paua muscle facing upwards, extract teeth from paua mouth by pushing into paua mouth with your thumbnails.

+ As you remove each paua from its shell and complete the first three steps, immediately place paua on a board and tenderise by banging once with the flat side of a meat mallet. Don't beat so hard that you break and tear the flesh. The paua are slippery and tend to fly around the kitchen during this process. To avoid this, encircle the paua as you go with a folded tea towel.

+ Clean shells of any remaining muscle, then wash and dry.

+ When you are ready to serve, heat a heavy-based frypan or flat grill plate and add a little clarified butter. Heat to medium-hot.

+ Place paua into frypan or on flat plate and cook for 1–1½ minutes on each side, or until lightly browned. Remove from pan and return paua meat to shells.

+ Squeeze lemon juice on each paua and season. Serve immediately with a cocktail fork and, if you wish, some thinly sliced, buttered white bread.

←

Salmon Tartare with
Lime Mayonnaise

Salmon Tartare with Lime Mayonnaise

MAKES 25 COCKTAIL SERVES

250g (¼) fillet fresh salmon
 (skin off and bone out)

1½ tblsp finely chopped chives

15ml (1 tblsp) sesame oil

30ml (2 tblsp) Tamari soy
 sauce

15ml (1 tblsp) rice wine vinegar

¼ tsp Maldon sea salt

⅛ tsp freshly ground black
 pepper

1 baby telegraph cucumber
 (very short julienne)

½ recipe Lime Mayonnaise
 (see page 189)

25–30g (5–6 tsp) salmon roe

extra chives for garnish

+ *This very refreshing salmon dish is shown in the photograph as I usually serve it – deconstructed. I'm giving you variations for presentation also. I dice the salmon one day ahead or on the morning of the party, and separately combine the marinade ingredients. I then combine the salmon with the marinade just before serving. I buy tiny telegraph cucumbers from Sue's Market Garden. They are very crisp and sweet, and as they are just baby cucumbers the seeds haven't yet formed.*

+ Cut salmon into 6mm dice.

+ In a non-reactive, medium bowl combine salmon, chives, sesame oil, soy sauce, vinegar, salt and pepper. Cover and refrigerate for up to 30 minutes, but no longer as the soy sauce and vinegar will break down the salmon.

+ Spoon salmon into one side of 25 cocktail-sized serving dishes. Place 4 or 5 pieces cucumber, a teaspoonful of Lime Mayonnaise and 4 or 5 salmon roe on the other side. If you wish, garnish with chives.

+ Serve with a cocktail fork.

SALMON TARTARE WITH LIME MAYONNAISE – VARIATIONS

SCALLOP SHELL

+ Into 25 queen scallop shells place a 3mm thick cucumber round. Top with some Salmon Tartare, then a dollop of Lime Mayonnaise. Garnish with salmon roe and a chive snip. Serve with a cocktail fork.

CHINESE SPOON

+ Into each of 25 Chinese spoons place 10g of Salmon Tartare. Place 4 or 5 pieces of julienned cucumber on the salmon, then a dollop of Lime Mayonnaise. Garnish with salmon roe and chives.

CUCUMBER WRAP

+ Using a mandoline or Rex peeler, very thinly slice a telegraph cucumber and cut into 13cm lengths. Season cucumber with salt and pepper. Sit slices between a paper towel for up to 30 minutes. Place a teaspoon of Salmon Tartare at one end of cucumber slice and roll up. If the cucumber is very thinly sliced each roll will stick without the use of a toothpick. Sit rolls upright and top with a little Lime Mayonnaise, some salmon roe and a chive snip.

SKEWERED

+ Thinly slice a cucumber using a mandoline or Rex peeler and cut into 13cm lengths. Season cucumber with salt and pepper and sit between paper towels. Thread one end of cucumber onto a skewer, followed by 4–5 cubes of Salmon Tartare. Finish by wrapping the remaining cucumber slice through the skewer and encasing the salmon. Use Lime Mayonnaise as a dipping sauce.

→

Parmigiano Gelato

Parmigiano Gelato

SERVES 10 FOR DRINKS

250ml (1 cup) cream

2 cloves garlic (peeled)

200g (3 cups + 1 tblsp) freshly grated Parmigiano-Reggiano

freshly grated nutmeg

freshly ground black pepper

+ *Cheese straws, gougères, Parmesan wafers and toasted cheese fingers are all delicious with champagne. Expect your friends to be surprised with this recipe when they discover that what is being served isn't ice-cream.*

+ Pour cream into a small, heavy-based saucepan. Add garlic and bring to the boil. Remove saucepan from heat and allow garlic to infuse cream for 30 minutes.

+ Bring cream back to the boil and remove garlic.

+ Reduce heat to as low as possible. I use a simmer mat to control the temperature underneath the pot. Add Parmigiano-Reggiano to scalded cream ½ cup at a time, stirring after each addition, until cheese is completely melted. Season with nutmeg and pepper to taste.

+ Pour mixture into a small but deep container and refrigerate until set, for at least 2 hours, but preferably overnight.

+ Once set and when ready to serve (allow Gelato to come to room temperature), use a small ice-cream scoop to ball the Gelato. Serve at room temperature, accompanied by Falwasser crackers, crusty French bread, cherry tomatoes, toasted walnuts, black olives or celery sticks.

CHRISTMAS DAY

When my sisters, my brother and I were kids, Mum and Dad used to put a pillowcase at the end of our beds for Father Christmas to fill with presents. Waking up on Christmas morning was so exciting for me that I still have precious memories of many Christmas mornings. Our pillowcases had small presents in them such as tennis balls, books, crayons, dolls' clothes, a beach towel, Jandals or shorts.

There were always nuts in shells that none of us ate, and an orange, which seemed odd to us because we thought oranges were not that special. But Mum and Dad were kids during the Depression and oranges would have been very special for them then. We would dutifully eat the orange – it was always an orange from Riverland, Australia, as my mother believed these to be the best oranges. And a very special food treat was a can of condensed milk each. John, my brother, worked out a way of prolonging condensed milk pleasure by making a hole in the lid with a hammer and nail, so we could drip feed ourselves until breakfast.

My father was a grocer, so the days leading up to Christmas were hectic for him. He had ham orders to fill and other deliveries to make right up to Christmas Eve, but we never felt he wasn't involved in our Christmas preparations. He would deliver to the Russian Embassy communal residence in Karori, and on Christmas Eve they always gave him a very strong bottle of vodka. And my mother would get red hopping mad if my father tried to palm off the shop leftover Christmas cakes to her. The cakes were made by the Magnet Bakery in Karori and by 24 December always had chipped icing and a well-worn Santa cake topper. Mum knew that her Christmas cake licked these shop jobs a hundred times over.

We always had a real Christmas tree, bought from the Scout Hall, and Dad would dress up as Father Christmas to hand out presents from under the tree – something he still does to this day. Around the tree were the major presents for each child, plus smaller ones from family friends or relatives.

The childhood Christmas morning thrill has long gone, and during fifteen years of working as a caterer I have woken up on Christmas morning simply feeling relieved I have actually lived until 25 December, and slightly disappointed that I have a day off but can't sleep in. But ask any chef and they will tell you they love to cook and entertain on Christmas Day. It is a very small gift you can give to your family, but very much appreciated by them all.

> We always had a real Christmas tree, bought from the Scout Hall, and Dad would dress up as Father Christmas to hand out presents from under the tree – something he still does to this day.

As a caterer, from May onwards I have been in Christmas mode planning menus for clients, pre-ordering turkey stocks and gearing our catering kitchen up during the quieter winter months to stockpile literally thousands of traditional but very special handmade Christmas cakes, so I am totally over turkey or Christmas pudding by about the middle of December and I don't fancy these Yuletide delicacies at home.

Many years ago I decided that a non-traditional Christmas dinner was the only way to go and I have now streamlined this to almost being 'Food in a Minute' – actually food in about thirty minutes. And three years ago I finally succumbed to an artificial Christmas tree. This was received with tremendous joy by Elaine Christensen, our housekeeper and decorator of Christmas trees. Elaine decorates the tree to a different theme every year, and we have a tree from mid-November onwards because clients begin to come to Springfield for Christmas parties from then. A real tree never lasts the distance so Elaine would end up decorating three trees rather than one – and having to clean up all the ensuing mess.

One year, Elaine and I sprayed key-ring whisks with gilt and hung them alongside dolls' house-sized saucepans on the tree – that was our kitchen theme. The following year I felt in a Chanel mood so we threaded strands of pearls through the tree, interspersed with big, flat, black velvet bows. My friend Clarence Chua suggested a marine theme and we spray-painted starfish in primary colours. Our most enduring theme is the tree Clarence created for our 'Traditional with a Twist' Christmas class. He sprayed agapanthus seed-heads red and a local sculptor, Debra Bustin, made angels with plastic forks as wings and Goldilocks pot cleaners as wigs. We hung one angel from the ceiling above the tree and a bevy of them dangled outside the front door.

On Christmas Day Paul and his son James are in charge of table setting, and they willingly move indoor furniture outside. I like an informal Christmas Day, but it has to be comfortable and civilised so I insist upon a padded chair. Hopefully I have had a tiny window of time the week before to make Christmas Mince Pies and Christmas Pudding Ice-cream. The window has been known not to open sometimes, so then I serve fresh raspberries with my old favourite,

Amaretto Dressing, which is in my first book, *The Best of Ruth Pretty*.

I begin the day sitting in the garden in my dressing gown with a latte and the outdoor speakers ringing loud with carols. We have raspberries, homemade muesli and runny cream for breakfast, even if we are having raspberries for Christmas dinner, and open our presents with a glass of champagne.

I then give some thought as to what pots and plates I will need for the feast to follow and also do whatever preparation is needed for the salads. James is an excellent helper and helps me to prepare the potatoes, beans and the live crayfish. All done in less than thirty minutes.

Paul's parents, Margaret and Harry, and my parents, Betty and Eric, arrive at midday and we begin the celebrations with champagne, nuts and muscatels. My sister and brother with their families, or Paul's brother with his family, may also join us. When we are all assembled, I ring my sister Anne in Turkey and we have turns at telling her what the weather is like.

We eat our Christmas dinner mid-afternoon, very leisurely, and with a good appetite. Everyone helps with the dishes, and by early evening we are onto coffee and ready for a relaxing night where no more food is required – and even an early night may be possible.

My nieces Cindy and Miranda Hill with my father, Eric Osboldstone ↓

←

Melissa's Barbecued
Salmon

SERVES 10–12

2 1kg salmon sides (skin on,
    bone out)

250ml (1 cup) Melissa's
    Barbecue Marinade (see
    below)

Italian parsley to garnish

lemon halves to garnish

Melissa's Barbecued Salmon

+ *I often serve this as an entrée on Christmas Day with thin slices
  of buttered Vogel's bread. When serving as a main course, I
  accompany it with minted potatoes and a green salad. Melissa
  is the daughter of some Portland, Oregon, friends and she cooked
  this dish for me at her house.*

+ Place salmon sides into a non-reactive gratin or flat dish. Pour half of
  the marinade over the salmon and rub into the flesh. Cover salmon and
  refrigerate overnight.

+ When ready to serve, preheat a barbecue flat plate to medium. When
  plate is hot, place 2 Teflon sheets on the barbecue and put 1 salmon
  side on each, skin-side facing upwards.

+ Cook salmon for 4–5 minutes before carefully turning salmon over. To turn
  over, fold a Teflon sheet over the salmon and with two pairs of tongs pick
  up all 4 corners to flip the salmon over.

+ Cook salmon for a further 4–5 minutes or until salmon is medium-rare,
  basting liberally with the remaining marinade.

+ Using Teflon sheets as a carriage, transfer salmon sides to a warmed
  platter carrier.

+ Remove Teflon sheets and garnish platter with Italian parsley and lemon halves.

MAKES 250ML

15ml (1 tblsp) olive oil

2 cloves garlic (peeled and
    finely chopped)

125ml (½ cup) Wattie's tomato
    sauce

60ml (¼ cup) Kikkoman soy
    sauce

30ml (2 tblsp) American
    mustard

10ml (2 tsp) Worcestershire
    Sauce (see page 187)

30ml (2 tblsp) lemon juice

½ tsp freshly ground pepper

75g (6 tblsp) sugar

Melissa's Barbecue Marinade

+ *Melissa specified ketchup in her recipe, but good old Wattie's
  tomato sauce does the same trick.*

+ Heat olive oil in a small non-reactive pot and when hot, add garlic.
  Cook over a gentle heat for 1–2 minutes without colouring.

+ Add the remaining ingredients and stir until the sugar is dissolved.
  Bring sauce to the boil and simmer for 15 minutes.

+ Allow to cool and refrigerate until required.

Christmas Day Crayfish with Minted Potatoes and Salads

SERVES 8

8 (400–600g) small live crayfish

+ *On Christmas Day it is essential to have small, freshly dug potatoes, which are perfect with simply prepared crayfish. I might also serve green beans, as well as two or three salads. This meal is so delicious that the thought of it carries me through those chaotic December days and nights when meals can become spasmodic.*

+ Drown crayfish in cold water and then plunge into a very large pot of boiling, lightly salted water.

+ Cook for 6–8 minutes, allowing 12 minutes per kg weight or until crayfish has turned a deep red colour.

+ Immediately drain crayfish into the kitchen sink, being careful not to break legs or feelers. Arrange on a large decorative platter and serve immediately. Alternatively, spread out on a big baking tray so they cool quickly, then refrigerate until required.

+ Serve outside with big napkins, lemons, sea salt, extra virgin olive oil, balsamic vinegar, mayonnaise, butter and a pepper mill. Allow guests to deal to their own crayfish.

+ Provide a decorative receptacle for guests to deposit crayfish heads and legs into and keep them to make crayfish stock.

→

Christmas Day Crayfish served
straight from the pot

Minted Potatoes

SERVES 10

1.5–2kg graded small
    potatoes (or allow 3
    potatoes per person)

small handful of mint

1 tsp salt

20g (2 tblsp) butter (diced)

Maldon sea salt and freshly
    ground black pepper

+ *I hardly need to give you a recipe for potatoes, but this is the foolproof method we use in catering. If you suspect the potatoes are not as sweet and creamy as you may like, add a tablespoon of butter to the potatoes as they cook.*

+ Peel or scrub potatoes, depending on quality.

+ Bring a large pot, half-filled with water, to the boil and add potatoes. Scoop out water until it is just even with the top of potatoes and add mint and a teaspoon of salt.

+ Replace lid on pot and bring to boil. Reduce to simmer with lid slightly ajar and cook for 10–15 minutes or until potatoes are just cooked or only just soft. Test with a metal skewer.

+ Pour off water and remove mint.

+ Add butter and seasoning to taste. To hold the potatoes until you are ready to serve them, cover them in the pot with a sheet of aluminium foil. Replace lid on pot and cover lid with a tea towel, tucking it into or around handle of pot.

+ If you have drained off all the water and captured steam in the pot, the potatoes will stay firm and hot for up to 30 minutes.

Tomato, Basil and Balsamic Vinegar Salad

SERVES 8

800g–1.6kg (8–16) tomatoes

24–48 basil leaves

16–24 cherry tomatoes

45ml (3 tblsp) extra virgin olive oil

30ml (2 tblsp) balsamic vinegar

Maldon sea salt and freshly
    ground black pepper

→

Tomato, Basil and
Balsamic Vinegar Salad

+ *I use red and yellow tomatoes in this salad. Every Christmas Eve, Sue from Sue's Market Garden gives me a carton, wrapped in Christmas paper, full of fresh garden produce. It is one of the highlights of all my Christmas gifts.*

+ Using a tomato or bread knife, slice tomatoes into 3 or 4 thick rounds, discarding the end pieces. If you are cutting tomatoes ahead of serving, arrange a paper towel on a plastic wrap-lined tray and stack tomato slices together as if they were still a whole tomato but lying on their sides end to end.

+ When ready to serve, layer tomato slices on a platter with basil leaves and strew with cherry tomatoes.

+ Drizzle with extra virgin olive oil and sprinkle with balsamic vinegar, and season just before you serve so you can still see salt flakes on the salad.

←

Avocado and Pink
Grapefruit Salad with
Purple Basil

Avocado and Pink Grapefruit Salad with Purple Basil

SERVES 8

4 avocados

juice of 1 lemon

4 (1–1.25kg) pink grapefruit
(also called ruby grapefruit)

24–48 purple basil leaves

Grapefruit Dressing (see below)

15–20 heartsease (pansies)

+ *The colours in this salad appeal to me greatly and, while I think it is a little corny to garnish with flowers, I adore the tiny purple and yellow heartsease on this salad.*

+ Cut avocados in half, stone and peel. Slice each avocado half into 3 or 4 slices and sprinkle with lemon juice.

+ Peel grapefruit using a small sharp knife, cutting peel off in strips from top to bottom and removing as much pith from the grapefruit as possible. Using a small serrated knife, segment the grapefruit, cutting down on either side of the membrane and retaining the excess juice.

+ On a large platter, alternate avocado slices and grapefruit segments, inserting purple basil leaves as you go.

+ Just before serving, drizzle salad with Grapefruit Dressing and sprinkle with heartsease.

Grapefruit Dressing

125ml (½ cup) extra virgin
olive oil

30ml (2 tblsp) grapefruit
juice reserved from
grapefruit segmenting

Maldon sea salt and freshly
ground black pepper

+ *On Christmas Day I go all out and use my favourite New Zealand extra virgin olive oils in my dressings. For this salad, I select an extra virgin olive oil with citrusy flavours rather than grassy flavours.*

+ Place oil in a bowl and pour in grapefruit juice as you whisk with a fork. Season to taste.

←

Christmas Pudding Ice-cream,
and Strawberries with Grappa

Christmas Pudding Ice-cream

SERVES 10–12

Custard Cream
(see page 106)

Whipped Cream
(see page 107)

Italian Meringue
(see page 107)

+ *For fun I sometimes serve this pudding flaming: invert the pudding onto the presentation tray, insert half a washed and dried eggshell into the top of the ice-cream pudding, pour a small amount of baby-bottle-warm brandy into the eggshell and light the brandy. Serve immediately.*

To assemble

+ Line a 2-litre bowl with plastic wrap.

+ Fold the cooled Custard Cream into the Whipped Cream and then fold the Italian Meringue into the custard mixture.

+ Pour ice-cream into prepared bowl. Cover and freeze overnight, or for up to one week.

+ Unmould when ready to serve. If you wish, drizzle with chocolate sauce, or sprinkle with shaved chocolate and/or serve with berries.

↑
Windsor Park is renowned in
our area for its berry fruit

100g (½ cup) raisins (firmly
    packed)

100g (½ cup + 2 tblsp)
    currants

100g (½ cup) sultanas (firmly
    packed)

50g (½ cup) dried apricots
    (finely chopped and firmly
    packed)

50g (⅓ cup) dried figs (stalks
    off, finely chopped)

250ml (1 cup) dark rum

8 egg yolks

40g (4 tblsp) castor sugar

8g (1 tblsp) icing sugar

62.5ml (¼ cup) Marsala

185ml (¾ cup) dry white wine

Custard Cream

+   *This is the base for the ice-cream, and to this you are going to fold
    in Whipped Cream followed by Italian Meringue (see opposite page).*

+   Place raisins, currants, sultanas, apricots and figs with rum into a bowl
    suitable for the microwave. Heat on medium until rum and fruits are just
    warm. Remove from heat and leave to soak for at least 30 minutes, or
    overnight if you wish.

+   Combine egg yolks, castor sugar and icing sugar in a bowl and mix with
    a wooden spoon until yolks become pale yellow. Do not beat in an electric
    mixer because you will create too much air. Add Marsala and wine and stir
    to combine.

+   Drain the fruit, reserving the rum for another use and add fruit to egg mixture.
    Stir to combine. Transfer to a heavy-based pot.

+   Cook over a low heat stirring constantly with a wooden spoon. When it is
    quite thick and like custard, and the mixture coats the wooden spoon,
    immediately transfer to a cold bowl and leave to cool.

Whipped Cream

500ml (2 cups) cream
20g (2 tblsp) castor sugar
16g (2 tblsp) icing sugar

+ Whip cream with sugars until a soft consistency is reached. It should just hold its peaks.

Italian Meringue

½ cup (4) egg whites at
 room temperature
20g (2 tblsp) castor sugar
 Syrup (see below)

+ Whisk egg whites very briefly until they just start to foam, then very slowly add the castor sugar, whisking all the time. Whisk until egg whites are stiff.
+ Very slowly and in a thin stream, begin pouring cooled Syrup into the beaten egg whites, continuously whisking. Whisk until all the Syrup is incorporated.

Syrup (for Italian Meringue)

105g (½ cup) castor sugar
125ml (½ cup) cold water
squeeze lemon juice

+ In a small pot combine sugar, water and lemon juice.
+ Place over a low heat, stirring until sugar is dissolved.
+ Increase the heat to medium and, without stirring, simmer until the syrup has even-sized bubbles across the surface. Don't allow the syrup to colour. Brush the pan with a wet pastry brush above the syrup level to remove crystallizing sugar as it bubbles.
+ Remove from heat.
+ Leave to cool slightly.

Strawberries with Grappa

SERVES 6

500g strawberries (hulled and
 halved)
105g (½ cup) castor sugar
juice and zest of 1 large lemon
30ml (2 tblsp) grappa or more
 to taste

+ *Christmas Day isn't complete without berries. This is the adult way of eating strawberries. Grappa is a colourless Italian eau de vie, distilled from the grape skins and seeds left as residue in the wine press.*
+ Place strawberries, sugar, juice and zest into a bowl. Mix well and set aside, stirring occasionally, until the sugar has melted.
+ Sprinkle with grappa and serve.

→
Baby Christmas
Mince Pies

Baby Christmas Mince Pies

MAKES 36 BABY MUFFIN-SIZED PIES

2 balls Sweet Short Pastry
(see page 186)

1 recipe Fruit Mince
(see below)

1 egg yolk

15ml (1 tblsp) water

+ *This is a particularly tasty version of Christmas mince pies, so it is worth investing the time to make them. I have them handy for when guests arrive for a drink or coffee before and after Christmas.*

+ Spray or grease 36 baby muffin tins.

+ Roll out each ball of pastry to 2mm thick. Using a 6.5cm frilly cookie cutter, cut out pastry bases and line baby muffin tins. Use pastry off-cuts to create stars for pie tops.

+ Preheat oven to 190°C.

+ Fill the uncooked pastry cases with Fruit Mince and place pastry stars on top of the mince. Rest pies in the fridge for at least 30 minutes before baking.

+ Whisk together egg yolk and water and brush onto stars. Bake for 20 minutes or until pies are golden brown.

+ Cool and remove from tins. Store at room temperature in a covered container with wax paper between layers, or freeze until required.

*MAKES ENOUGH TO FILL 36 BABY
MUFFIN-SIZED PIES*

125g (½ cup + ⅓ cup) sultanas

125g (½ cup + ⅓ cup) currants

125g (½ cup + ⅓ cup) raisins

65g (½ cup) dates (softened
in hot water)

65g (½ cup) dried apricots

65g (⅓ cup) brown sugar

30ml (2 tblsp) brandy

125g bananas (1–2 bananas
mashed)

Fruit Mince

+ Place sultanas in a food processor fitted with a metal blade, and chop using the pulse button. Place sultanas in a bowl. Do the same with the currants, raisins, dates and apricots.

+ Add remaining ingredients to bowl and stir to combine.

+ Store in an airtight container in the fridge or in sterilised jars in a cool place.

BOXING DAY

On Christmas Day my father likes to suck, pull and squeeze every delicious skerrick of meat and juice from his serve of crayfish, and I am pleased to say he is the only guest to indulge in this primeval pastime. He becomes like a dog with a bone and of course it means there is one less crayfish head for my stockpot. After Christmas lunch I put all the pristine crayfish heads and bodies into a pot to make stock so visitors on Boxing Day can enjoy a comforting bowl of Crayfish Chowder.

Glass-fronted cupboards in the butler's pantry hold collections of useful food-related silver objects

Silver napkin rings from part of a large collection

When my kitchen was altered and extended, I decided that instead of a fridge I would have a small walk-in chiller, as I still had recurring nightmares of my Marbles Restaurant days where an inordinate amount of time was spent juggling fridge space because we didn't have a chiller. I figured that a walk-in chiller in my own kitchen would help me through that particular psychosis. My chiller has wooden shelves, a linoleum floor, a flat stainless-steel door, and on Christmas Day it's big enough to store all the leftovers. So when the crayfish stock has cooled, I leave it in the stainless-steel pot overnight in the chiller to strain the next day.

I can remember back to the early sixties when our family acquired its first fridge. We all oohed and aahed as it stood in the centre of the kitchen waiting for my father to lift it into its little place under the bench. It was short and squat, and these days would probably be considered a bar fridge.

Boxing Day is always the first day for a long time when I am able to have a smallish sleep in, but I actually like to get up early and begin reading whatever treasures I have been given for Christmas – and drink plenty of coffee. After my chiller, the second most 'can't live without' item in my kitchen is my espresso machine. My attempt at good home coffee began with an $89 plug-in job, which in hindsight was about as satisfactory at making espresso as the 1956 toy sewing machine I still own. I went up a notch to a $400 machine but hid it when guests arrived, as making more than one espresso was absurd. Then I finally took the plunge and purchased a Rocket machine, and I have never looked back. And one day I'll invest in a fully plumbed commerical machine.

Christmas Day is more about family than friends, so for me Boxing Day is friends' day. The only real household activity I like to get out of the way is rubbish removal. Crayfish remains, Christmas wrapping and wine bottles all go to the tip. On that trip Paul may stop at a few gardens to get whatever bits and pieces we might need for lunch. I am fairly organised though for Boxing Day and to accompany the Crayfish Chowder I have soft white rolls to bake waiting in the freezer. The fish that I purchased on Christmas Eve is in the chiller, portioned and ready to barbecue. And my favourite Boxing Day dessert, Mille-feuille, comes together with whatever fruit is left over from Christmas Day. Hopefully I have had time before Christmas to make the pastry cream filling, which I like to flavour with Grand Marnier, or another favourite liqueur of mine, Amaretto.

I have been known to make a creamy filling for Mille-feuille by folding thickened yoghurt into cream, then adding sugar and vanilla seeds. Sometimes I colour that by stirring in some strained raspberry purée. It gives you a different sort of Mille-feuille but is still very worthwhile. Pre-rolled puff pastry is always a good standby for the freezer, but I do prefer a commercial puff pastry made with butter and will roll this out on the day so the pastry is nice and fresh.

In our catering kitchen we make thousands of Christmas cakes so I can't be bothered with cake at home. Instead I make large quantities of Panforte, which I have usually given away to friends by the time Christmas comes. I attempt to have my Panforte made by the end of November; it doesn't improve with age but neither does it deteriorate.

After Boxing Day lunch, I encourage guests and dogs to take a big walk along the beach. If guests are staying for dinner I serve a 'clean out the chiller' version of Salad Niçoise. My post-Christmas chiller can produce minted baby potatoes, leftover beans, olives that someone has given me, cherry tomatoes and perhaps some leftover fish from lunch. If the fish has all been eaten then I have tins of tuna packed in oil in the pantry as a standby, and I always have fresh eggs to hard boil. I pour a big slug of local extra virgin olive oil and a drizzle of balsamic vinegar over the salad, prepare for an early night – and then onwards with summer.

Boxing Day is always the first day for a long time when I am able to have a smallish sleep in, but I actually like to get up early and begin reading whatever treasures I have been given for Christmas – and drink plenty of coffee.

←

Crayfish Chowder

Crayfish Chowder

Crayfish Chowder

MAKES 1 LITRE, TO SERVE 4

1 litre (4 cups) crayfish stock

50g butter

1 clove garlic (finely chopped)

140g (½ cup) large onion (finely diced)

100g (½) red pepper (finely diced)

100g (½) yellow pepper (finely diced)

75–100g (1 stick) celery (finely diced)

50g (½ cup + 3 tblsp + 2 tsp) flour

125ml (½) cup cream

few drops Tabasco

30ml (2 tblsp) lemon juice

Maldon sea salt and freshly ground black pepper

1 cooked crayfish tail (meat removed and cut into medallions)

2 tblsp chopped chervil or Italian parsley

4 lemon halves

+ *Sometimes I make a scallop or scampi chowder with fish stock rather than crayfish stock. I use some additional fish stock to poach scallops or scampi tails, which I then float in the chowder.*

+ Place stock in a saucepan over a high heat. Bring to the boil then reduce to a simmer. Cook until stock has reduced by 25 per cent to 750ml.

+ Melt butter in a medium saucepan and add garlic, onion, peppers and celery. Sauté over a medium heat until vegetables are tender but not browned. This will take about 10 minutes.

+ Add flour and stir 3–4 minutes until butter and flour smells nutty (this is the roux).

+ To the roux slowly add reduced crayfish stock, stirring constantly until smooth.

+ Simmer gently for 5–10 minutes.

+ Add cream, Tabasco, lemon juice and seasonings to taste.

+ Ladle hot chowder into serving bowls and top each serving with a cooked crayfish medallion, a sprinkle of chervil or Italian parsley and a lemon half on the side.

Crayfish Stock

MAKES 1.625 LITRES

15g (1 tblsp) butter

150–170g (1) leek (white portion only, finely chopped)

150–170g (1) large carrot (finely chopped)

75–100g (1 stick) celery (finely chopped)

250–270g (1) large onion (finely chopped)

1kg (3) crayfish heads and bodies

250ml (1 cup) white wine

2.5 litres water (or to cover)

1 sprig thyme

1 bay leaf

few stalks parsley

+ *Thirty minutes is really the maximum cooking time for any sort of seafood stock. It will smell and taste very bitter and fishy if it is overcooked.*

+ Lightly butter bottom of a saucepan.

+ Place vegetables in the saucepan first and then crayfish heads and bodies on top.

+ Cover pan and place over a low heat. Slowly cook ingredients until vegetables soften and sweat. This will take at least 10 minutes.

+ Add wine and water to cover.

+ Without a lid, bring to boil and remove scum as it forms on top. Add herbs to stock. Turn stock to a medium heat and simmer for 30 minutes.

+ Let cool and strain through a fine sieve, or better still a sieve lined with muslin.

Soft White Dinner Rolls

MAKES 20

+ Using Burger Bun recipe on page 59, form dough into 20 40g pieces and shape into balls.

+ If you wish, glaze tops with egg yolk mixed with a little water and sprinkle with sesame seeds.

+ Bake rolls according to instructions for 12 minutes or until golden brown and cooked through.

→
Barbecued Groper with Tomato Basil
Salad and Sherry Vinegar Butter Sauce

Barbecued Groper with Tomato Basil Salad and Sherry Vinegar Butter Sauce

SERVES 8 AS A MAIN COURSE

8 160–180g groper pieces

30ml (2 tblsp) olive oil

Tomato and Basil Salad
(see page 119)

Sherry Vinegar Butter Sauce
(see page 119)

8 lemon wedges

+ *Groper is also called hapuka and is one of my most favourite fish. Its firmness makes it an excellent barbecuing fish.*

+ Preheat the barbecue flat plate and line with a Teflon sheet. A Teflon sheet is invaluable when barbecuing fish as the fish never sticks to the Teflon, whether skinned or not, and is also suitable to combat the stickiest of marinades.

+ Coat groper in oil and place on barbecue.

+ Cook 3–4 minutes each side or until cooked through.

+ Remove from barbecue. Cover with aluminium foil to keep fish warm and place away from the heat.

+ Divide Tomato and Basil Salad evenly between 8 serving plates. Place groper on top of salad and top with a spoonful of Sherry Vinegar Butter Sauce.

+ Serve with a wedge of lemon.

←

I like to decorate with vegetables as well as flowers

SERVES 8

160–180g (16) red cherry tomatoes (halved)

160–180g (16) yellow cherry tomatoes (halved)

65ml (¼ cup) extra virgin olive oil

1 tsp Maldon sea salt

¼ tsp freshly ground black pepper

24 basil leaves

Tomato and Basil Salad

+ *This is a very simple salad, but is a perfect base to support the flavours of Barbecued Groper and Sherry Vinegar Butter Sauce.*

+ In a small bowl combine tomatoes, oil, salt and pepper. Set aside for 30–60 minutes for flavours to infuse.

+ Up to 5 minutes before serving add whole basil leaves and stir well to coat.

MAKES 170ML

375ml (1½ cups) chicken stock

185ml (¾ cup) sherry vinegar

20g (2 tblsp) butter (cubed)

45ml (3 tblsp) lemon juice

½ tsp Maldon sea salt

⅛ tsp freshly ground black pepper

Sherry Vinegar Butter Sauce

+ *Make sure you use a sherry vinegar from Spain. Anything other than Spanish sherry vinegar will not cut the mustard.*

+ In a small saucepan combine stock and vinegar.

+ Place over a high heat and boil until reduced to 125ml (½ cup). Remove from heat.

+ Whisk in butter 1 tablespoon at a time until sauce is glossy. Stir in lemon juice, salt and pepper.

+ Taste for seasoning and serve hot or warm.

→
Summer Mille-feuille

Summer Mille-feuille

SERVES 8–10

Puff Pastry Rectangles
    (see opposite page)

1 recipe Crème Patisserie
    (see opposite page)

250g (3 cups) strawberries
    (cut into halves or quarters)

300ml cream (whipped)

300g (2¾ cups) berries
    (raspberries, loganberries, etc)

Brulée Sugar Crystals
    (see page 45)

+ *This is a particularly luscious version of a custard square and you can vary this recipe to make it as long and as spectacular as your imagination will allow.*

+ Place one Puff Pastry Rectangle on a wooden board or large flat platter suitable for presentation. Using a palette knife spread 1½ cups Crème Patisserie over pastry.

+ Sprinkle strawberries on Crème Patisserie and top with second Puff Pastry Rectangle.

+ Combine cream with remaining Crème Patisserie and spread on second Puff Pastry Rectangle and sprinkle with berries.

+ To complete the Mille-feuille, add the final Puff Pastry Rectangle and just before you serve, sprinkle with Brulée Sugar Crystals.

+ Caramelise the top of the Mille-feuille using a brulée torch (or alternatively place the pastry sheet under a hot grill prior to assembling the final stage).

Puff Pastry Rectangles

500g puff pastry

flour for dusting

30g (2 tblsp) butter (melted)

45g (6 tsp) sugar

+ *One thing I don't make at home is puff pastry. Sometimes I use pre-rolled puff pastry but I prefer a very good commercial puff pastry which is made with butter rather than lard or margarine.*

+ Preheat oven to 200°C.

+ Cut pastry into three equal pieces and place on a floured bench.

+ Roll out each pastry sheet into a large rectangle (35 x 18cm) and neaten by using a small knife to trim the edges to make a 33 x 16.5cm rectangle. Place on a baking tray and rest in refrigerator for 15 minutes. Repeat the process for the remaining pieces of puff pastry.

+ Pierce the rectangles all over with a fork, brush with melted butter, sprinkle with sugar and bake in oven for 15–20 minutes until golden brown and completely cooked.

+ Transfer to a cooling rack and use when completely cold. Alternatively, store in an airtight container until ready to use.

Crème Patisserie

MAKES 600ML

1 vanilla bean (split in half)

500ml (2 cups) milk

250g (1¼ cups) sugar

60g (⅓ cup + 2 tblsp) flour

6 egg yolks

45ml (3 tblsp) Grand Marnier

+ *This thickened custard is a useful filling for tarts, filled cakes, or choux pastries. Ring the changes by folding in melted chocolate, espresso or raspberry purée to taste.*

+ Heat vanilla bean and milk in a saucepan on medium heat and bring to the boil.

+ In a bowl whisk together sugar, flour and egg yolks until pale. Slowly pour milk into egg mixture, whisking continuously as you pour.

+ Transfer mixture to a saucepan and stir over a low heat until mixture comes to the boil, then simmer for 2 minutes. The mixture should be thick and custardy.

+ Pour mixture through a sieve into a clean bowl, using a soup ladle to help you push it through the sieve. Reserve vanilla bean for another use.

+ Fold in the Grand Marnier, then cool to room temperature. Cover with plastic wrap on top of mixture, rather than covering bowl, and place in refrigerator until completely cold.

+ This will keep for several days in the refrigerator but does not freeze well.

←

Panforte

Panforte

MAKES 36 PIECES

140g (1 cup) blanched
  almonds

140g (1 cup) hazelnuts

125g (¾ cup + 3 tblsp) flour

12g (2 tblsp) cocoa

5g (1 tblsp) cinnamon

5g (1 tblsp) mixed spice

200g (1¼ cups) dried apricots
  (chopped)

150g (1 cup) Lexia raisins
  (chopped)

zest of 1 orange

zest of 1 lemon

60ml (¼ cup) brandy

155g (¾ cup) castor sugar

125g (⅓ cup) runny honey

icing sugar for dusting

+ *This is my version of the sweetmeat delicacy from Sienna in Tuscany. It keeps extremely well when stored airtight in the pantry.*

+ Preheat oven to 180°C. Spray a 25cm round non-stick tin and line base with baking paper, or better still with a Teflon sheet.

+ Roast almonds and hazelnuts in oven for 5–7 minutes and roughly remove skins from hazelnuts.

+ Sift flour, cocoa, cinnamon and spice into a bowl and add nuts, apricots, raisins and zests, then add brandy.

+ In a small saucepan over a low heat stir sugar and honey until the sugar is dissolved. Increase heat, bring to the boil and simmer for 1–2 minutes until bubbles are formed which are even across the surface, i.e. until syrup reaches soft ball stage. To test for soft-ball stage, fill a saucer with cold water and put in a drop of syrup. If it coheres the syrup is at soft-ball stage.

+ Quickly add hot syrup to nuts and fruit. This step is easily done using an electric mixer fitted with the paddle attachment.

+ Pour some water in a small bowl and dip your fingertips in and out of the water as you press mixture into the prepared tin, smoothing the surface as you go. Bake for 35–40 minutes or until Panforte springs back slightly to the touch.

+ Allow Panforte to sit for 10 minutes before turning out onto a cooling rack. Remove baking paper or Teflon and let cool completely. Slice into thin wedges and dust with icing sugar.

+ Store in an airtight container. When serving, redust with icing sugar if you wish.

GRAZING

When we first owned Springfield we had a constant stream of visitors, as friends were curious to see what we had bought. The first few years we were only here at weekends, and major earthworks seemed to take place most Saturdays or Sundays. The trailer-loads going to the tip were never-ending and friends had no choice but to work alongside us.

↑ Sophie

In those days I had a dog called Brandy, who was a black spoodle (a cross between a spaniel and a poodle), adopted rather than stolen from my next-door neighbour when I lived in Kelburn, Wellington. She visited me daily for several years until she finally moved in, with my neighbour's consent. Brandy was there in the early years of Springfield for every tree fell, afternoon tea and swim in the stream when the weather got so hot it became unbearable. She is now buried beside the cottage in the garden.

When we first arrived at Springfield the cottage was a large shed divided into two rooms, close to the house. In one room there were old leather suitcases, stacks of fading newspapers and lots of empty cartons. In the other smaller room were tools, a hand lawn-mower and some old paint cans. On one wall of this small room,

etched with pencil on the rimu, was a stock list of jams and jellies – Gooseberry Jam, Crabapple Jelly, Elderflower Jelly, Blackberry Jam – all marked January 1908.

One weekend Paul decided to move the shed. So instead of facing the house, it now opens out into the garden and doesn't block the sunlight from the end of the house. The food store is now a bunk-room, still with the etching, and the bigger room is a guest cottage, affectionately known as the bridal suite, where a bridal couple may spend their first night after their celebration at Springfield.

These days we give our guests the weekend off from gardening and use the two days as an opportunity to relax as well. From Springfield, a short drive east takes us into the hills and the Otaki Forks, which is a Department of Conservation camping area and entrance to tramping tracks in the Tararuas. There you can swim in the Otaki River or take bush walks and talk to cheeky wood pigeons.

I also take visitors to the market gardens to meet the growers, buy vegetables for dinner and for them to stock up their car boot for the return home. It always surprises me how many children haven't seen apricots on a tree or tomatoes on a vine. If you think children don't like eating greens, then watch them scoff down beans they pluck themselves.

A long beach walk is wonderful in the late afternoon, as the sunsets on Te Horo Beach are magnificent. Kapiti Island looks different in every light and it is easy to feel the mysticism of local legend. And on the low tide, we collect baskets of pipis or tuatuas, which I then leave to spit sand overnight in a bucket of water. Pipi or tuatua fritters, barbecued with little sausages from the local butcher and served with bacon

and tomatoes, are a first-class brunch for guests. If you have caught, gathered or picked what you eat, it will always taste better, and of course the story of the chase gathers momentum with every mouthful.

Back home, our Rhode Island Reds give us plenty of farm-fresh eggs. They eat our scraps and some from the commercial kitchen, so the yolks of their eggs are rich and tasty. Brunch will often be Scrambled Eggs with tarragon from the garden, or Poached Eggs with chopped coriander and slugs of Tomato Chilli Jam. For children visiting, it has to be Buttermilk Pancakes with Apple Syrup and Crispy Bacon or Pancakes with Raspberries, which I semi-crush into the batter.

Early risers at our place make their own tea and toast, or enjoy some fresh local fruit. Brunch does away with the midday lunch ritual, but in the afternoon guests can become peckish. I might then serve afternoon tea, late afternoon dessert,

It always surprises me how many children haven't seen apricots on a tree or tomatoes on a vine. If you think children don't like eating greens, then watch them scoff down beans they pluck themselves.

early pre-dinner drinks, mid-afternoon wine tasting or a late light lunch. These meals are more than snacks; they are little occasions in themselves which can while away afternoons, along with reading, talking, dozing and walking.

After Brandy I thought there wouldn't be any more dogs at Springfield, but eventually Bud and Casey came to live. One day, my nephew Matthew and I took one of our Peking ducks with a broken leg to the vet. The vet put the duck's leg in a splint, and then took us out to his back doorstep to show us a proud Dad, their family pet, a Keeshound or Dutch Barge dog. The Keeshound had mated with their Huntaway, the farm dog used for rounding up sheep. Dad was attending to the litter of eight while Mum continued working, just returning for feeding. Naturally we took a puppy home

↑ The swing on Walnut Island

with us. She looked very much like a frightened possum and we called her Bud. Matthew named her after a friend's Mum he was particularly fond of at Playcentre, who was also called Bud.

Casey arrived at two years old, a pedigree pug from Raglan, whose bloodline had outstayed its welcome at the kennels. Like all pugs, Casey hated being alone and the first night he whimpered in the laundry until he was allowed into the bedroom. But Paul decided Casey and Bud should sleep in a kennel, so we had a magnificent kennel built. However, Casey became sadder by the day in the kennel and his curled tail hung to the ground. The vet diagnosed cancer and issued a death warrant for him, but we refused to sign it and for supper gave Casey a miniature Moro bar. He perked up. So every day for the next ten years we gave him a small chocolate bar and let him sleep in our bedroom until he died at nineteen. He is buried next to Brandy, and Bud is buried on Walnut Island at Springfield.

The Mangione Stream runs through our garden, and an island has been created in an area where the stream has forked. Wild walnut trees grow there, so we call it Walnut Island. It is a special part of the garden where no one thinks to look for you. During Brandy's days, we installed a curved bridge to the island, because I was besotted with curved bridges. Clare, our wonderful gardener, has planted the Wedding Day rose on the island side of the bridge to ramble up into the trees and along the sides of the bridge.

I often pack a picnic and we move en masse to Walnut Island. My friend Sarah Hodge, who lives close by in Manakau at her nursery, Horrobin and Hodge, would take her children on a camping holiday to

↑ Our neglected pear orchard

across the road where they live. Thomas and Ella never understood how far or how little they had travelled. For all they knew they could be anywhere. That's how I feel when I have a picnic on Walnut Island.

Our present dogs, Sophie and Ellie, trail us all around the garden. Sophie, in particular, enjoys afternoon tea, so for a special treat I give her a saucer of milky sweet tea. Sophie retired here when she was ten and, being a French poodle, is very particular about what she eats. She is very disdainful of Ellie, who is a sweet little girl pug, but like all pugs has no manners when it comes to eating.

I always enjoy the time with my friends at Springfield, whether on the verandah, on Walnut Island, in the gazebo, on the seating we built around the giant totara tree or on the stony beach of the stream.

←

Smoked Oyster Butter with
Vogel's Toast Rounds

MAKES 12 TOASTS

85g (1 tin) smoked oysters
(drained)

100g butter (diced and
softened)

Maldon sea salt and freshly
ground pepper

2–3 drops Worcestershire
Sauce (see page 187)

juice of ½ lemon

12 Vogel's Toast Rounds
(see page 188)

Italian parsley for garnish

zest of 2 lemons

Smoked Oyster Butter with Vogel's Toast Rounds

+ *This is one of my standby recipes – very tasty with a drink. Smoked oysters are always handy to have in the pantry.*

+ Place smoked oysters in a bowl and mash with a fork.

+ Add butter, salt, pepper, Worcestershire Sauce and lemon juice to taste.

+ Thickly butter Vogel's Toast Rounds with oyster mixture.

+ Alternatively, serve in a small jar accompanied with Vogel's Toast Rounds and sliced cucumber.

+ Garnish with Italian parsley and lemon zest.

+ Serve immediately.

→

Pork Pies with Tamarillo Chutney

Pork Pies with Tamarillo Chutney

MAKES 24 BABY MUFFIN-SIZED PIES

2 recipes Short Pastry (see page 186)

1 recipe Pork Pie Filling (see opposite page)

egg wash (1 egg yolk mixed with 1 tblsp water)

375ml (1½ cups) Pork Stock (see opposite page)

Tamarillo Chutney (see page 187)

+ *To prepare lunch-sized pies, you will need 1 recipe rather than 2 recipes of pastry. Make 4 lunch pies in deep dishes such as custard cups, ramekins or teacups, 175ml in volume; this will give you a traditional-looking raised pie. The pies can be made up to two days in advance or frozen.*

+ Preheat oven to 190°C.

+ Prepare muffin tins by spraying or greasing well. Roll pastry on a floured bench to 2mm thickness.

+ Using a 7.5cm frilly-edged cutter, cut 24 bases for pies. With a 5cm frilly-edged cutter, cut 24 tops. Push bases into prepared baby muffin tins. Cut a 5mm round hole in the centre of each pastry top.

+ Fill bases with pork mixture to about ¾ full.

+ Using a small pastry brush, brush under-side of tops with water and place on top of filled bases. Press the edges together with a fork. Rest pies for 20 minutes in refrigerator, then brush tops with egg wash.

+ Bake in oven for 17–20 minutes until pastry is golden brown. Cool.

+ Pour stock into a squeeze bottle, then squeeze enough stock into each pie through the hole in the top to come up to the top of the pie. Refrigerate pies until stock has jellied.

+ Serve Pork Pies at room temperature, accompanied by Tamarillo Chutney.

Pork Pie Filling

MAKES 24 BABY MUFFIN-SIZED PIES

320g pork fillet (silverskin removed)

10ml (2 tsp) olive oil

90g (1 small) onion (finely diced)

3 tblsp finely chopped fresh sage

1 tblsp finely chopped fresh thyme

Maldon sea salt and freshly ground pepper

+ Cut pork into 0.5cm cubes.

+ Preheat a heavy-based frypan and smear with oil. Add pork to pan and sear quickly on all sides. Reduce heat, add onion and cook until onion is soft and pork is cooked through.

+ Remove from heat, add herbs to pan and season with salt and pepper.

+ Refrigerate or freeze for future use.

Pork Stock

MAKES 650ML

1.3kg pork spare ribs

240g (2) red onions (washed and cut into quarters)

350g (2) carrots (washed and roughly chopped)

250g (1) leek (washed and roughly cut)

3 litres water (or enough to cover bones and vegetables in pot)

3 celery stalks (washed and roughly cut)

1 bay leaf

6 peppercorns

bunch of thyme

+ *You may consider life is too short to make pork stock, in which case use a can of chicken or beef consommé in the Pork Pie recipe. However, remember to reduce it as per the final instruction in this method. Skimming is an important part of the process of making a good stock. It prevents any impurities from boiling back into the stock, thus producing a clear and flavoursome liquid. It is also important to simmer rather than boil, as boiling will cause the stock to become cloudy.*

+ Preheat oven to 200°C.

+ Place pork bones in a large roasting tray and roast for 25–30 minutes, or until lightly browned.

+ Add onions, carrots and leek to roasting tray and cook for a further 20–30 minutes or until vegetables are lightly browned.

+ Transfer contents of roasting tray to a large pot. Over medium heat, pour a little boiling water into roasting tray and with a fish slice remove any sediment which has formed on the bottom. Add this liquid to the pot and cover contents of pot with cold water.

+ Bring pot to the boil and add remaining ingredients. Return to the boil and simmer uncovered for 3–4 hours, skimming stock whenever necessary.

+ Strain stock through muslin placed over a sieve, then cool.

+ The following day, remove fat from top of the stock and discard. Proceed with next step or refrigerate. Alternatively, freeze stock in small plastic containers or ice cube trays until ready to use.

+ Before using, place pork stock in a saucepan, bring to the boil then reduce heat and simmer until stock has reduced by half.

→

Variety of squashes displayed at
Philip and Sue Sue's stall. I use
them for cooker and decoration

Summer Mélange of Melon, Pepper and Mint

SERVES 6–7

250g (½) rockmelon (peeled,
seeded and cut into bite-
sized pieces)

70g (½) red pepper (deseeded
and cut into 5mm strips)

35g (¼) yellow pepper
(deseeded and cut into
5mm strips)

75g green grapes (destalked)

40g (½ medium) red onion
(peeled and finely sliced)

40g (2–3 medium-sized)
radishes (trimmed and
finely sliced)

30ml (2 tblsp) extra virgin
olive oil

30ml (2 tblsp) balsamic vinegar

handful fresh mint leaves
(chopped)

Maldon salt and freshly ground
black pepper

+ *This is an extremely fresh, moreish salad. Serve with a glass
of herbaceous New Zealand sauvignon blanc for a grazing-
style late lunch. It can be made up to one day in advance,
leaving the mint to add when you serve, but it is best made
on the day it is to be eaten.*

+ Place all ingredients in a bowl and gently combine.

+ Cover and refrigerate until required.

←
Piquant Figs, Feta and
Crispy Prosciutto Salad

Piquant Figs, Feta and Crispy Prosciutto Salad

SERVES 8

75g (3–5 slices) prosciutto
(sliced)

8 large handfuls baby salad
greens

1 recipe Red Wine and Honey
Dressing (see below)

1 recipe Piquant Figs (see below)

150g feta (cut into 1cm cubes)

+ *A very suitable grazing salad as it gets your taste-buds going.
It works well as a snack, an entrée, for lunch with baguettes
and apples, or as an accompaniment to roast chicken.*

+ Preheat oven to 200ºC.

+ Place prosciutto between two layers of baking paper. Place in oven
for 8–12 minutes until crispy and golden. Cool.

+ In a bowl place baby salad greens. Drizzle with Red Wine and Honey
Dressing and toss.

+ Scatter Piquant Figs, feta and prosciutto over the top and serve immediately.

Piquant Figs

115–125g (16) dried figlets
(stems trimmed)

10g (8) whole almonds
(toasted and cut lengthwise
in half)

1 tsp freshly cracked black
pepper

5 bay leaves

+ *These figs will keep in the jar for months and make a much
appreciated gift, provided you tell the receiver their uses.
A bowl of Piquant Figs with the dressing drizzled over them
makes a moreish addition at drinks' time alongside bowls
of cherry tomatoes and marinated feta cubes.*

+ Cut each figlet through the centre, leaving the stem end intact.

+ Gently push one almond half into the cut edge of one half of each figlet.

+ Push the two halves of the figlet together to enclose the almond.

+ Sprinkle figlets with pepper.

+ Layer figlets and bay leaves in a clean glass jar, seal tightly and store
in a cool dark place for up to 1 week before using.

Red Wine and Honey Dressing

20g (1 tblsp + 1 tsp) runny honey

30ml (2 tblsp) red wine vinegar

¼ tsp finely chopped fresh thyme

+ In a small bowl combine all ingredients and whisk well.

 →
Baby Bagels with Smoked
Salmon and Cream Cheese

Baby Bagels with Smoked Salmon and Cream Cheese

MAKES 30 FILLED COCKTAIL BAGELS

30 cocktail-sized bagels
   (see opposite page)

450g cream cheese

200g smoked salmon
   (or 15 slices)

squeeze of lemon

grind of pepper

lamb's lettuce, rocket or
   endive if desired

+ *Fingerfood is perfect grazing material and Bagels with Smoked Salmon and Cream Cheese are always enjoyed with coffee at any time of the day or with a casual drink. You can fill them several hours ahead and refrigerate them until required.*

+ Cut bagels in half and generously spread cream cheese on each cut side.

+ Top each bottom half with a slice of smoked salmon and add a squeeze of lemon juice and a grind of pepper.

+ Place some salad greens, e.g. rocket or lamb's lettuce, on top of salmon.

+ Place top half of bagel on salmon and salad greens.

+ Place filled bagels in an airtight container in fridge until ready to serve. Layer wax paper in between bagels.

Baby Bagels

MAKES 30 COCKTAIL-SIZED BAGELS

10g (1 tblsp) yeast

10g (1 tblsp) sugar

62.5ml (¼ cup) warm water

560g (4 cups) high grade flour

15g (1 tblsp) salt

20g (2 tblsp) sugar

1 egg yolk

62.5ml (¼ cup) warm water

125ml (½ cup) warm milk

50ml (3 tblsp) salad or
    vegetable oil

extra oil for greasing rising
    bowl

extra yolk and 1 tblsp water
    for glaze

poppy or sesame seeds

+ *I make a batch or two of these and keep them in plastic bags in the freezer at all times. Usually I fill them with smoked salmon, but sometimes I use ham or roast beef. They can also be enjoyed at brunch with cream cheese and raspberry jam.*

+ In a small bowl mix yeast with first measure of sugar and water. Cover with plastic wrap and leave for 5–10 minutes until yeast mixture becomes foamy.

+ In an electric mixer or food processor place flour, salt and second measure of sugar.

+ In another bowl whisk egg yolk with second measure of water, and milk and oil.

+ Pour yeast mixture on flour and process or mix briefly.

+ With mixer or food processor running, pour in egg yolk mixture and combine until a stiff dough forms. The mixture may need up to ¼ cup of additional warm water.

+ Knead dough in mixer with dough hook, or remove from food processor and knead on bench until dough is soft and pliable. (Kneading the dough in the food processor will make the dough tough.)

+ Brush a china or glass bowl with extra oil and place dough into bowl to rise. Cover with plastic wrap and place bowl in a warm place until dough doubles in size. Preheat oven to 200°C.

+ Roll out dough to approximately 1cm thick and cut out with a cocktail-sized, bagel-shaped cutter. If you use a bagel cutter you will have dough remaining, so leave remaining dough for second rising and then re-roll out and cut bagels as above. Alternatively, divide dough into 30 balls and roll each piece into a sausage with your hands. Wet one end with cold water and then join the two ends together so you have a circle with a hole in the middle.

+ Before you bake bagels, you need to poach them. Place bagels on a greased baking tray and stand tray in a warm place for about 10 minutes.

+ Bring a wide frypan of water to the boil and drop some bagels into the pan. Don't crowd the pan.

+ Using a slotted spoon, turn bagels over after 1 minute. Wait another minute and remove bagels from the pan back onto the greased tray.

+ Lightly whisk extra egg yolk and water, and quickly brush tops of bagels.

+ Sprinkle bagels with poppy or sesame seeds.

+ Bake at 200ºC for 15–20 minutes or until golden brown.

+ Serve immediately or store until later in the day. Alternatively, freeze bagels free flow, then store in plastic bags until you are ready to use. They take a very short time to thaw at room temperature.

Potato-top Meat Pies with Worcestershire Sauce

MAKES 8 8CM LUNCH-SIZED PIES

400g puff pastry

20g (2 tblsp) butter

100g (1 small) onion (finely diced)

1 clove garlic (finely chopped)

80g (½ medium) carrot (peeled and finely diced)

80g (10–15) button mushrooms (destalked and diced)

30ml (2 tblsp) oil

500g ribeye steak (diced)

25g (2½ tblsp) butter

50g (⅓ cup less 1 tsp) flour

200ml (¾ cup + 1 tblsp) beef stock

75ml (¼ cup + 1 tblsp) Mac's Gold beer

30ml (2 tblsp) Worcestershire Sauce (see page 187)

few drops Tabasco sauce

Maldon sea salt and freshly ground black pepper

Mashed Potatoes (see below)

90g (1 cup + 5 tblsp) freshly grated Parmesan cheese

Worcestershire Sauce, extra

+ *Pack warm into paper bags and take to a picnic not far from your kitchen, with a bottle of Worcestershire Sauce in hand.*

+ Grease or spray 8 lunch-sized pie dishes measuring 8cm in diameter. (You will find aluminium pie dishes in your supermarket.)

+ Roll pastry to 2–3mm thickness, or alternatively buy pre-rolled pastry, and using a 17cm round cutter (or a side plate) press out 8 rounds.

+ Gently press pastry into pie dishes, making sure pastry touches base and comes right to the sides of the pie dishes. Rest in refrigerator for 20–30 minutes while making filling.

+ Melt butter in a heavy-based frypan, add onion and sauté over a medium heat until onion is golden in colour but not browned.

+ Add garlic and cook for a further minute. Add carrot and mushrooms and cook a further 3–4 minutes until carrot is beginning to soften and mushrooms are soft. Tip into a bowl and set aside.

+ Add oil to the same frypan, and when hot sear the beef in two batches. Then set beef aside.

+ Melt second measure of butter in a medium-sized saucepan. Add flour and cook, stirring occasionally, for 2–3 minutes, or until butter and flour becomes a nutty brown colour.

+ Slowly add stock and beer, constantly stirring, until roux is smooth and thickened. Add Worcestershire Sauce, Tabasco, salt and pepper. Stir to combine and simmer over a low heat for 2–3 minutes. Taste for seasoning.

+ Remove from heat and add beef and vegetables to sauce. Cool. Preheat oven to 200°C.

+ Spoon cooled filling into rested pie bases. Top with Mashed Potatoes and sprinkle each pie with Parmesan. Store in refrigerator or bake immediately.

+ To bake, place pies in oven and cook for 30–35 minutes until pastry is golden brown and cheese is just colouring.

+ Serve with Worcestershire Sauce.

Mashed Potatoes for Potato-top Pies

ENOUGH TO TOP 8 8CM PIES

750g potatoes (peeled and chopped)

25g (2½ tblsp) butter (diced)

30ml (2 tblsp) cream

1 egg yolk (beaten)

freshly grated nutmeg

Maldon sea salt and freshly ground black pepper

+ *For very fluffy mashed potatoes use the Moonlight variety.*

+ Steam potatoes until tender, then place potatoes in a bowl and mash.

+ Add butter, cream, half of egg yolk (discard other half), nutmeg, salt and pepper to taste, and with a large fork beat potatoes until smooth and fluffy.

←

Chocolate Baklava

Chocolate Baklava

MAKES 123CM SQUARE, 18 PIECES

85g (¾ cup) unsalted
   pistachios

110g (¾ cup) blanched
   almonds

185g dark chocolate (finely
   chopped)

150g figs (very finely chopped)

1½ tsp cinnamon

¾ tsp cloves

zest of 1 orange

100g butter (melted)

28 filo pastry sheets

1 recipe Orange Syrup
   (see page 188)

+ *Serve this delight in the late afternoon with coffee. It is rich but worth every calorie.*

+ Place nuts in a food processor and pulse until medium to finely chopped. Tip into a bowl and add chocolate, figs, cinnamon, cloves and orange zest. Combine well, then divide mixture into three.

+ Using a pastry brush, butter bottom and sides of a 23cm-square baking dish.

+ Place filo pastry sheets on a flat surface and cut the stack so the width equals 23cm. Cover pastry with a slightly damp cloth to prevent it drying out while you work.

+ Place a filo pastry sheet on a flat surface and brush with butter. Repeat the process until there are 10 buttered sheets in a stack. Lift pastry sheets and place into baking dish covering the base, with the excess coming up the sides.

+ Sprinkle ⅓ of chocolate mixture evenly over the surface of the pastry.

+ Cut remaining filo pastry sheets into 23cm square sheets. Brush 2 sheets with butter. Repeat this process and place these 4 sheets on top of the chocolate mixture.

+ Sprinkle the second third of the chocolate mixture on the pastry. Repeat the process using another 4 sheets of filo and the remaining chocolate mixture.

+ Place the remaining 10 filo pastry sheet squares on top of the chocolate mixture, brushing butter on every second layer including the top.

+ Trim any excess pastry from the sides of the tin so the pastry is level and neat. Cover with plastic wrap and chill in the refrigerator for at least 30 minutes or up to 2 hours.

+ Preheat oven to 180°C.

+ Remove Chocolate Baklava from refrigerator and, leaving it in the baking dish, cut it into 9 even-sized squares, then cut each square into 2 triangles. You can cut each triangle in half again to make 36 petit four-sized pieces. Brush top layer with melted butter.

+ Bake in oven 35–40 minutes or until golden in colour.

+ Remove Chocolate Baklava from oven and pour cooled Orange Syrup evenly over the top (some will run into the cuts but do not deliberately pour into the cuts). Allow Chocolate Baklava to stand and absorb the syrup for at least 2 hours before serving.

+ Store covered at room temperature.

→

Honey Almond Slice

Honey Almond Slice

BASE:

100g butter (melted)
165g (⅔ cup + 3 tblsp) sugar
160g (1 cup + 3 tblsp) flour
55g (½ cup) ground almonds

TOPPING:

125g butter (roughly diced)
85g (¼ cup) honey
135g (1⅓ cups) flaked almonds

+ *This recipe originally came from my friend and colleague, Dianne Kenderdine. I cut it into small squares and serve any time, but it goes particularly well with tea. The flavours are complex without being overly rich or even sweet, and it freezes well.*

To make the base:

+ Preheat oven to 180ºC. Spray and grease a sponge roll tin or a slice tin measuring 30cm x 21cm or alternatively line with Teflon paper.

+ Combine all ingredients in a bowl and using the K beater of an electric mixer, or a wooden spoon, mix ingredients together. Press base evenly into the bottom of prepared tin.

+ Bake for 15 minutes or until mixture is cooked through and lightly golden in colour. Cool slightly.

To prepare the topping:

+ Place butter and honey into a heavy-based saucepan and stir over a medium heat until butter is melted.

+ Increase heat and cook butter mixture until small bubbles appear evenly across surface, or a sugar thermometer reads 115ºC (or soft-ball stage). Remove from heat and stir in almonds, then spread over base.

+ Return tray to oven and cook a further 15 minutes or until golden brown.

+ While slice is still warm, cut into squares or bars. Store in an airtight container with waxed paper between each layer.

Melon and Champagne Ices

130g (⅔ cup) sugar

125ml (½ cup) water

30ml (2 tblsp) lemon juice

250ml (1 cup) champagne

½ rockmelon (peeled, deseeded, puréed and sieved to make 250ml/1 cup)

¼ watermelon (peeled, deseeded, puréed and sieved to make 250ml/1 cup)

30ml (2 tblsp) cognac (iced)

30ml (2 tblsp) gin (iced)

←

Melon and
Champagne Ices

+ *This is not as creamy and firm as a sorbet, but has the texture of granita. Enjoy it on a hot afternoon or accompany it with raspberries for a refreshing dessert. You may like to reserve the melon shells and freeze them to be used as serving vessels.*

+ Boil sugar and water together, then leave to cool thoroughly.

+ Combine syrup with lemon juice and champagne. Divide mixture in half.

+ Add puréed rockmelon to one half and puréed watermelon to the second half.

+ Pour into ice-cube trays and freeze, loosening the mixture from the sides with a fork and stirring from time to time as it freezes.

+ Once rockmelon mixture is frozen, tip into an iced serving bowl or rockmelon shell. (Work it a bit with a fork if too firm as it should be slightly mushy.) Add cognac and mix well.

+ Once watermelon mixture is frozen, tip into an iced serving bowl or watermelon shell. (Work it a bit with a fork if too firm as it should be slightly mushy). Add gin and mix well.

+ Return the ices in bowls (or shells) to the freezer for 2–4 hours.

+ Serve directly from iced serving bowls (or shells), or for individual serves fork into shooter glasses.

+ Ices can be stored in a sealed container for up to 10 days, but the flavour does begin to diminish.

CAKES

Catering is all about moving from one crisis to another, and the more experienced you become, the stronger you are at coping with crises. Nowadays, what seems like a crisis to anyone else is part and parcel of what I have come to expect. An everyday critical moment inhouse is called a CC or catering crisis. Higher up the scale is a CCC, which is a catering cake crisis.

Many years ago while still a wet-behind-the-ears caterer, I was asked to cater for a christening party. It was to be fingerfood and champagne, presented late morning. The occasion was to be formally acknowledged an hour or so into the party with toasts and the cutting of the christening cake, which, after much discussion, was to be a round, graduated, three-tiered sponge cake, each tier sitting directly on top of the other. The cakes were to be layered with fresh cream and strawberries, and the tiers covered in Italian meringue frosting. The florist rang me several weeks ahead to confirm the circumference of each tier as Cécile Brünner roses and tweedia were to be entwined as wreaths around the cake.

With christening cakes, and all cakes, I have always believed that taste should come first. And I thought this particular cake would only be delicious if it was filled with fresh cream on the day. The christening was in February and the day dawned very hot and humid. I duly filled the cakes and began work on the Italian meringue frosting, which incidentally I had never made before. It seemed to work perfectly and the cake was covered in shiny, white-peaked frosting and looked spectacular. However, it did take longer than I anticipated, but I quickly packed it into a crate and off we all went in the van. On the way to Wellington there was an accident at Pukerua Bay stopping the traffic. We sat in the van for thirty minutes, opening the windows for respite against the heat.

And so with the accumulated loss of time we arrived one and a half hours later to the house than planned, just as the family, with baby wrapped in an antique white shawl, was arriving back from the church. My old friend Jo Boyer was to be in charge out front and she immediately swung into action

to make up for our late arrival. She began to unload the van and, from the word that she uttered, I knew we had a CCC on our hands – and it was a major one.

Because of the humidity and heat, and my unskilled preparation, the egg white and syrup in the frosting had separated and the egg white had descended to the base of the cake, sitting there idle like sea foam. The syrup had nowhere to go except into the sponge and the three tiers had become dislodged from each other. To top it off, the cream had also curdled. Jo, like a matador enticing and protecting herself from a prize bull, flicked open a big, white, linen tablecloth and, before our clients came into view of the offending object, pronounced to the mother and baby that she was covering the cake to keep the surprise intact.

We dramatically carried the cake inside to the kitchen, then shut ourselves and the cake in the pantry. In fearful whispers we agreed that Jo had to carry on with service

Mothers also began to interrupt by passing me baby food to microwave, and the last straw was a toddler under my feet eating tinned cat food out of the pet bowl. It had rapidly become the kitchen from hell ...

and I would prepare food in the kitchen and also try to remedy the cake. We explained to the hostess that fashion dictated it was sacrilege to stop the flow of savoury passarounds for the cake cutting, and recommended that the formal part of the ceremony should be later than originally planned.

Suddenly, Jo now needed more trays of food to serve just as some small children entered my zone demanding juice. Mothers also began to interrupt by passing me baby food to microwave, and the last straw was a toddler under my feet eating tinned cat food out of the pet bowl. It had rapidly become the kitchen from hell but just as I was about to succumb to failure, my adrenalin kicked in when a mother pulled on the pantry door where the cake was hidden, anxious to procure a biscuit for her child. In one movement I dragged her off, thrusting a cocktail-sized Florentine into her hand.

I then dispatched Sarah Mortimer, Jo's helper, on a mission to return with twelve punnets of cream cheese and a bag of icing sugar. She had to go to three supermarkets as this must have been the last day in the area before the cream cheese delivery.

I found the food processor, bemoaning the fact that it was an itsy bitsy teenie one. In between filling, cooking and garnishing fingerfood, and washing silver platters, I made load after load of cream cheese frosting in the food processor. Sarah's next job was to pick ivy, and when she politely inferred that this wasn't an option as the ivy was growing over a precipice, I managed to coerce her by explaining that what looked like a cliff was an illusion, a bit like a mai mai.

I moulded the three tiers into a disparate shape with my hands, and convinced myself that the curdled cream would be mistaken

for ricotta. The cake was totally skew-whiff,
but I patched up cracks and crevices with
cream cheese frosting before I smothered
the monster with more frosting and randomly
criss-crossed ivy around and over it. I
deconstructed the florist's wreaths and
hung them loosely from the top of the
cake like maypole strands.

Jo and I took very deep breaths to gather
up our remaining strength and, with an aria
playing from *La Traviata*, we dramatically
and ceremoniously carried the edifice into
the sitting-room. The room gasped, then
clapped and cheered. Shona MacFarlane,
the well-known New Zealand artist, was a
guest and begged me to let her take a
photo, declaring that it was an inspirational
work of art.

The baby is now fourteen years old, and
I still can't look his mother in the eye.

If you follow the recipes in this chapter
and allow yourself ample time, you will have
magnificent results worthy of a memorable
celebration.

→

Oscar Lloyd decorating the Chocolate
and Almond Celebration Cake

Chocolate and Almond Celebration Cake

+ *This Celebration Cake is moist and rich, and remains this way for at least a week. And it freezes well if there is any left over. With correct construction it is strong enough to withstand travel, which makes it a caterer's best friend. It is made up of three round cakes, graduated in size, and each one is filled and coated with Ganache Soufflé. Then the three cakes are stacked directly on top of each other and drizzled and iced with Ganache. Accompany with fresh raspberries.*

INGREDIENTS FOR CELEBRATION CAKE

1 20cm Chocolate and Almond Cake and cake board (see page 152)

1 25cm Chocolate and Almond Cake and cake board (see page 152)

1 30cm Chocolate and Almond Cake and cake board (see page 152)

Ganache Soufflé (see page 153)

Ganache (see page 153)

flowers, ribbons, candles, sparklers or ornaments of your choice

+ Remove cakes from tins and peel away baking paper. Place each cake on a flat baking tray and using a bread knife cut each one in half horizontally to form two layers. Starting with the smallest cake, slide a second baking tray between the two layers and lift off the top layer.

+ Spread the top side of top layer with Ganache Soufflé and top with bottom layer of the cake turned upside down. (The top of the cake is not usually smooth so use the bottom, i.e. the edge that sat next to the cake tin.)

+ Repeat this with the remaining 2 cakes.

+ Place each cake onto a thin, aluminium-foil-covered cake board, 3cm in diameter less than the cake diameter. It is important for the final presentation that all cakes are even in height, so measure and trim accordingly.

+ Apply a thin layer of Ganache Soufflé to the top and sides of each cake. This is called the crumb layer as it prevents cake crumbs from going into the final layer of Ganache. (It must be applied as carefully as the Ganache layer because it is the base on which the Ganache sits.)

+ Line the tray or cake stand you intend presenting the Celebration Cake on with 20cm squares of greaseproof paper. Place them so they appear diamond-shaped and overlay top corners. (This paper provides a Ganache splash guard for the presentation tray or cake stand.)

+ Place the 30cm cake with the cake board on the tray or cake stand. Poke 3 wooden meat skewers into the cake and mark skewers level to the cake – remove them and cut at the marked point. These will act as support for resting the cake above on.

+ When the skewers are the correct height place them back into the cake. Top the 30cm cake with the 25cm cake with the cake board. Repeat the process with 3 meat skewers, making sure the skewers are placed within the diameter of the cake board beneath each cake. Top with the 20cm cake. Skewers are not required in this top tier.

+ Look at the 3-tiered cake from all angles to ensure the 3 tiers are level. Adjust if necessary by lifting the lower edge of a cake and packing it with a little Ganache Soufflé. You are now ready to ice with Ganache. →

→

Chocolate and Almond
Celebration Cake

+ Pour Ganache over the top tier and let it drip down the sides of each cake. On the small ledge created between each tier run your palette knife (a flexible, long, thin, metal spatula) around in a horizontal position to smooth the icing. Do not be tempted to apply water or heat to the palette knife or the Ganache.

+ Using a palette knife, and holding it against the side of the cake in an upright position, move around the cake smoothing the Ganache as evenly as possible. Repeat with all the cakes. (A cake turntable makes this part easy so that the cake turns rather than you.)

+ If the Ganache is at the correct temperature, the top of the top tier will be perfect. If the Ganache was a little thick when you applied it, it will not sit smoothly so use a palette knife and move in a circular motion around the cake to smooth the top. (Once again, do not be tempted to apply water or heat to the palette knife or the Ganache.)

+ Leave in a cool, dry place for Ganache to set. This Celebration Cake can be made a day or two ahead and stored in a cool dry place. (Do not be tempted to put in the refrigerator, as this will make the Ganache weep. In particularly warm weather place in a small draught, for example, near a partially opened window.)

+ Gently remove greaseproof paper from the presentation tray or cake stand. Decorate as you please and serve that day, or within the next two days.

Chocolate and Almond Cake

+ *I make these cakes in an electric mixer, one at a time. Alternatively, use a large bowl, mix by hand and make one at a time. I prefer to work with chocolate buttons (but not chocolate melts) as they are more convenient, but you can cut chocolate slabs into small pieces. Use the best quality chocolate you can afford. High grade flour is available at supermarkets and is stronger than standard flour.*

1 20CM ROUND CAKE

250g (1½ cups + 1 tblsp) dark chocolate buttons (or slab chopped)

65ml (¼ cup) dark rum

30ml (2 tblsp) strong coffee

250g unsalted butter

6 eggs (separated)

250g (1¼ cups) castor sugar

125g (½ cup + ⅓ cup + 1 tblsp) high grade flour (sifted)

125g (1 cup + 1 tblsp) ground almonds

1 25CM ROUND CAKE

415g (2½ cups + 1½ tblsp) dark chocolate buttons (or slab chopped)

110ml (¼ cup + 3 tblsp) dark rum

50ml (3 tblsp + 1 tsp) strong coffee

415g unsalted butter

10 eggs (separated)

415g (2 cups less 1 tsp) castor sugar

210g (1½ cups) high grade flour (sifted)

210g (1¾ cups) ground almonds

1 30CM ROUND CAKE

580g (3½ cups + 2 tblsp) dark chocolate buttons (or slab chopped)

155ml (½ cup + 2 tblsp) dark rum

70ml (¼ cup + 1 tsp) strong coffee

580g unsalted butter

14 eggs (separated)

580g (2¾ cups) castor sugar

295g (2 cups + 2 tblsp) high grade flour (sifted)

295g (2½ cups) ground almonds

+ Preheat oven to 150°C. Spray the sides and bases of cake tins and line each base with baking paper. The tins need to be a minimum of 7cm deep.

+ Melt chocolate, rum and coffee over a double boiler, making sure that the water under the chocolate pot doesn't boil and/or steam is not falling back into the chocolate. Alternatively melt in microwave on medium, stirring every minute. Cool.

+ Cut butter into cubes and soften in microwave.

+ Lightly beat egg yolks.

+ Place butter into the bowl of an electric mixer and add sugar. Using the K beater, beat until butter and sugar is creamed, i.e. pale yellow and slightly fluffy.

+ Pour cooled chocolate mixture and egg yolks into butter and beat until combined. At this point, for the 30cm cake transfer mixture to a larger bowl than the bowl of your electric mixer.

+ Place sifted flour into mixture and then add ground almonds. Stir until just combined.

+ In another bowl, with a clean dry whisk, whisk egg whites until soft peaks form. Using a metal spoon, gently fold egg whites into chocolate mixture. Aim to have egg whites still visible in the mixture.

+ Pour mixture into prepared tins.

+ Bake 20cm cake for around 1 hour 20 minutes, 25cm cake for around 1 hour 40 minutes, and the 30cm cake for around 1 hour 50 minutes. Test to see if cakes are cooked by inserting a metal skewer. The cake is a moist, dense cake so when it is cooked the skewer will come out with tacky mixture attached to it. The cake will not spring back when prodded as it has a crusty top.

+ Cool tins on a cake rack. Remove cakes from tins when totally cold.

Ganache and Ganache Soufflé for a Chocolate and Almond Celebration Cake

MAKES 3.45 LITRES

1.8 litres (7 cups + 3 tblsp + 1 tsp) cream

1.8kg (11¼ cups) dark chocolate (buttons or slab roughly chopped into small pieces) (I use Belgian chocolate – do not use chocolate melts)

+ *Ganache is a rich chocolate icing made from chocolate and cream that is heated and stirred until the chocolate has melted. The mixture is then cooled until lukewarm and poured or spread over a cake so it becomes the icing on the cake. Ganache Soufflé is made from the same base, also cooled but then whipped to approximately twice its original volume and is used to fill cakes.*

+ Pour cream into a large pot and bring to a temperature just below boiling. Remove from heat.

+ Add chocolate and using a metal spoon stir gently until all the chocolate has melted and Ganache is smooth. If you whisk or stir vigorously, or use a wooden spoon, you will create air bubbles which will appear as tiny pits in the Ganache when it is set.

+ Cool Ganache to just about cold. You can place it in the refrigerator very briefly.

+ Measure 1.3 litres of Ganache and reserve in refrigerator to chill so you can make Ganache Soufflé for the filling. Leave the remaining Ganache, which should measure 2.15 litres, at room temperature as it will become the icing. When Ganache is ready to be used as icing, it will be silky and of a thick pouring consistency.

+ For Ganache Soufflé, beat the Ganache set aside for Ganache Soufflé with an electric mixer, or whisk, until mixture is creamy and stiff. (Don't over-beat Ganache Soufflé as it can curdle.) Use immediately while it is flexible enough to spread.

Ganache and Ganache Soufflé for Individual Chocolate and Almond Cakes

+ *You may want to present a single-tier Chocolate and Almond Cake instead of the three-tier Celebration Cake. In the following table I have given you the quantities for Ganache and Ganache Soufflé for the 3 sizes of cakes. As they will be solo cakes, the Ganache quantity given allows for complete coverage of a cake. The total volume column indicates the volume when chocolate has melted into cream. The total volume is then divided, so that you have mixture to make into Ganache for icing and Ganache Soufflé for filling.*

CAKE	20cm ROUND	25cm ROUND	35cm ROUND
CREAM	*400ML*	*550ML*	*650ML*
CHOCOLATE	*400G*	*550G*	*650G*
TOTAL VOLUME	*750ML*	*1 LITRE*	*1.2 LITRES*
GANACHE	*450ML*	*550ML*	*650ML*
GANACHE SOUFFLÉ	*300ML*	*450ML*	*550ML*

Perfect-in-Pink Cake

Ella Horrobin pleased to receive
a Perfect-in-Pink Cake

Perfect-in-Pink Cake

Firm Sponge Cake
  (see page 157)

4 tblsp Raspberry Jam
  (see page 188)

Marshmallow Round
  (see page 157)

In-the-Pink Icing
  (see page 157)

hundreds and thousands

+ *My friend Ella Horrobin loves cooking, sewing and making things. She sends me presents of painted and ribboned little boxes filled with handmade truffles or delicate little tussie mussies made with flowers and herbs from her parents' nursery garden, Horrobin and Hodge. Ella's favourite colour is pink and I made this cake in her honour. It is a cake very suited to a little or big girl's birthday, and it is beautiful presented wrapped in tulle.*

+ When sponges are completely cold turn them upside-down and spread with Raspberry Jam.

+ Place Marshmallow Round on one cake directly on top of Raspberry Jam. Top with the remaining sponge, Raspberry Jam-side directly on Marshmallow Round.

+ Ice cake with In-the-Pink Icing and decorate using hundreds and thousands. Make a template of a name, age, heart or flower and sprinkle hundreds and thousands on the template.

+ Serve cake on the day of baking preferably, although it can still be enjoyed one or two days later.

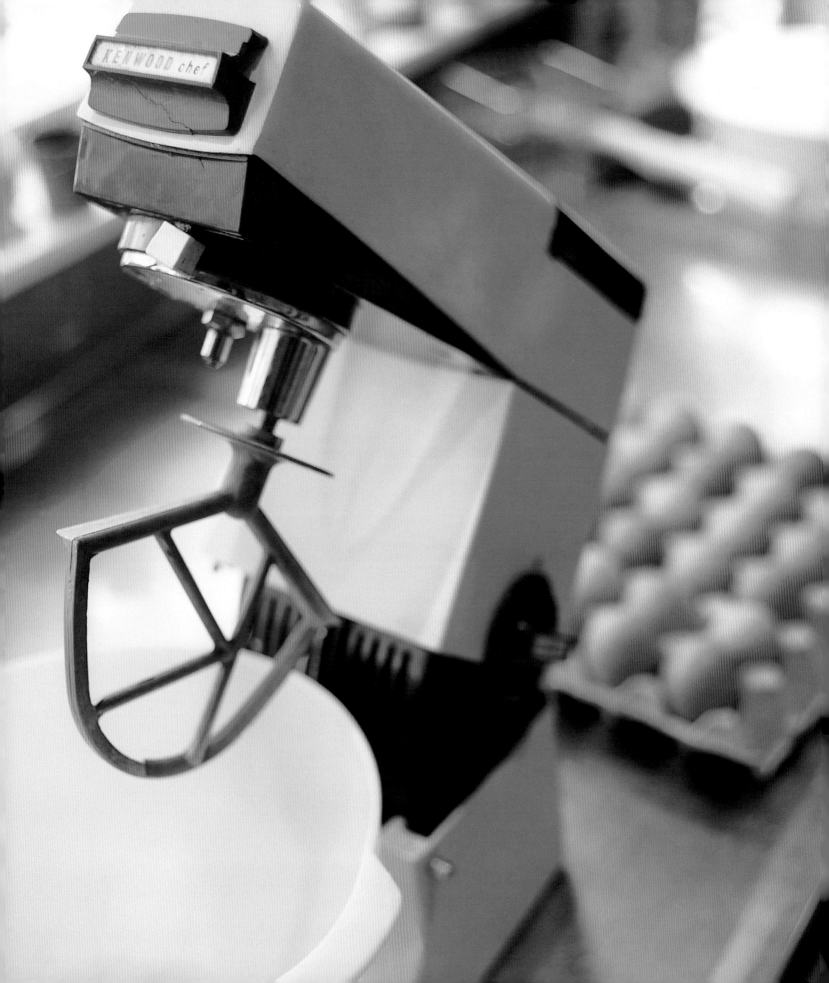

←
I love my Kenwood mixer which I bought second-hand and have owned for many years

Firm Sponge Cake

+ *These are shallow cakes individually, but in a sandwich with the Marshmallow Round you end up with a high cake. This is a very useful sponge generally for layering.*

MAKES 2 17CM ROUND CAKES

3 eggs

pinch salt

175g (¾ cup + 2 tblsp + 1 tsp) sugar

50g butter (chopped)

30ml (2 tblsp) boiling water

125g (¾ cup + 3 tblsp) flour

5g (1 tsp) baking powder

+ Preheat oven to 180°C. Grease 2 17cm round cake tins and line bases with baking paper.

+ Place eggs, salt and sugar in a bowl and whisk until thick and pale yellow.

+ Add butter to boiling water and stir until butter is melted.

+ Sift flour and baking powder and fold into egg mixture, alternating with butter/water mixture.

+ Pour batter into prepared tins. Bake for 15 minutes or until surface of sponge pops back when you prod it.

+ Remove from oven and leave to cool for 10 minutes before turning out onto a cake rack.

Marshmallow Round

MAKES 1 17CM ROUND

1½ tsp cornflour

1½ tsp icing sugar

12g (1 tblsp) gelatine

62ml (¼ cup) water

200g (1 cup) sugar

125ml (½ cup) water

1 tsp vanilla essence

1 drop red food colouring

+ Grease a 17cm round tin, (base and sides). Sift cornflour with icing sugar and sprinkle into tin. Shake tin to give a light all-over coating and tip out any excess.

+ Place gelatine and first measure of water in a small bowl. Stir and leave for 10 minutes or until gelatine has absorbed the water.

+ Place sugar and second measure of water in a small pot. Heat gently, stirring constantly with a metal spoon until sugar dissolves.

+ Place bowl of gelatine over a small pot of hot water and stir gelatine until it dissolves. Pour gelatine into sugar mixture and bring to the boil. Boil steadily for 15 minutes. Allow to cool until lukewarm.

+ Pour gelatine mixture in a large bowl, add vanilla essence and food colouring to mixture and stir until combined. Whisk, (preferably with an electric mixer) until very thick. Pour into prepared tin and leave to set for at least 2 hours, or until set. Do not store in the refrigerator.

In-the-Pink Icing

150g (1 cup) icing sugar, sifted

5g (1 tsp) butter (softened)

25ml (5 tsp) hot water

1 drop red food colouring

+ Place icing sugar, butter and hot water into a small bowl and beat with a wooden spoon until smooth.

+ Add food colouring and stir until combined.

←
Chocolate Strawberry Tower

Chocolate Strawberry Tower

Chocolate Strawberry Tower

*MAKES 30–40 DESSERT SERVINGS
OR 70–80 SERVINGS WITH COFFEE*

1.8kg (11¼ cups) dark
chocolate buttons (or slab
chocolate chopped into
small pieces but do use
chocolate melts)

5.5–6kg (155–180) long-
stemmed strawberries

+   *This is splendid served with New Year's Day drinks, for a
    dessert party on Christmas Eve or as a Wedding Celebration
    Cake. For the quantity of chocolate and strawberries used in
    this recipe, you will need a 44cm-high croquembouche mould
    with a base diameter of 23.5cm. The strawberries must be
    first-grade, large strawberries, picked dry, and dipped when
    very fresh. If they are at all damp, the liquid will seep through
    the chocolate. Use the best chocolate you can afford.*

+   Melt chocolate, preferably using the double boiler method. Be careful not
    to get water in the pot underneath the chocolate pot too hot, or to allow
    steam to fall back into the chocolate. If using a microwave, heat chocolate
    for 1 minute on medium, remove and stir. Repeat until chocolate is melted.

+   Dip half to three-quarters of each strawberry in chocolate and place on
    baking trays lined with aluminium foil.

+   Place trays preferably in freezer, or in refrigerator, for 2–3 minutes or until
    chocolate is firm.

+   Place a 44cm-high croquembouche mould with a base diameter of
    23.5cm onto a presentation tray. I like to use an upturned round antique
    silver tray with a slightly larger diameter than the diameter of the base of
    the croquembouche mould.

+   Take each dipped strawberry one at a time and, using a small palette
    knife (a long, thin, flexible metal spatula), dab a little of the remaining
    melted chocolate onto the lower side edge of the strawberry. Place the
    strawberries to sit glued both onto the tray and the croquembouche
    mould. Continue with dipped strawberries to make a single layer around
    base of mould.

+   Continue up the mould, sitting strawberries on top of each other and filling
    in the gaps between strawberries with smaller strawberries to ensure you
    cover all the mould.

+   Once you reach the top, choose 3–5 very good-looking strawberries to
    sit on the flat top of the mould for a glamorous finish to your Chocolate
    Strawberry Tower.

+   Serve as soon as possible. If you have to store it for a few hours, leave in
    a cool, dark place. And if the weather is hot or humid, leave in a draught.

→

Jo-Anne Tracey's Carrot Gateau

Jo-Anne Tracey's Carrot Gateau

SERVES 14–16

420g (2 cups) castor sugar

315ml (1¼ cups) salad oil

10ml (2 tsp) pure vanilla essence

2 tsp finely grated lemon rind

3 eggs (lightly beaten)

270g (2 cups) carrots
 (peeled and grated)

195g (1 cup) apple
 (peeled and grated)

250g (1 cup) unsweetened
 crushed pineapple (drained)

65ml (¼ cup) pineapple juice
 (juice from crushed pineapple)

40g (½ cup) desiccated coconut

420g (3 cups) flour

1 tsp cinnamon

2 tsp baking soda

½ tsp salt

+ *This is the best carrot cake I have ever tasted. Jo is the Ruth Pretty Catering chef in charge of recipe testing, and she loves to entertain at home. When you live in the country you expect weekend visitors, and this cake is a specialty of the Tracey household.*

+ Preheat oven to 170°C. Spray and flour a 25cm diameter, 7.5cm deep ring tin.

+ In a large bowl whisk together sugar, oil, vanilla and lemon rind with a hand whisk. Do not use an electric mixer as you will create too much air.

+ Add eggs and mix well. Stir in carrot, apple, pineapple, pineapple juice and coconut.

+ Sift dry ingredients, add to bowl and gently fold in.

+ Pour batter into prepared tin and bake for approximately 1 hour or until a cake skewer inserted comes out clean, and the cake bounces back when prodded.

+ Allow cake to cool in the tin for 10 minutes, then remove cake from tin to a cooling rack to cool completely.

+ Ice with Cream Cheese Frosting.

Cream Cheese Frosting

TO ICE 1 25CM CAKE

375g (1½ cups) cream cheese

30ml (2 tblsp) lemon juice
 (juice of 1 lemon)

1 tblsp + 1 tsp zest of 1 lemon

10g (1 tblsp) butter (diced and
 softened)

375g (2½ cups) icing sugar
 (sifted)

+ *A peaky cream cheese frosting is too sweet for me. I prefer a citrusy flavour as in this recipe, and I don't mind if it sits smooth and flat.*

+ In a medium-sized bowl beat cream cheese until smooth and creamy.

+ Add lemon juice, zest and butter and combine well.

+ Add icing sugar and beat until combined and frosting is smooth.

WEDDINGS AT HOME

Paul's first job, aged eleven, was packing tomatoes for Penny and Ray Bertlesen at Penray Gardens, one of the largest and longest-standing market gardens in this area. The Bertlesen children began to arrive on the scene during Paul's first year in the shed. Ray's son, Brent, and his wife, Jane, run the gardens today. Rochelle is Penny and Ray's only daughter, and on Saturday 21 April 1990 Ray was a very proud father of the bride as he made his welcome speech to the guests assembled in the marquee on our front lawn – the first wedding to be held at Springfield.

→

A very simple cermony table set up near the stream

We served the wedding guests a buffet dinner that featured Suckling Pig, and from that day onwards I became a devout believer in serving suckling pigs or lambs at wedding feasts. They are festive and communal, and the guests are driven wild by such an alluring aroma as the animals turn on the spit. The bountifulness of serving a whole animal is summed up by the old saying: For you I would have killed the fatted calf. Though I am yet to roast a calf.

The locals have told me about the wedding of one of the Tolhurst daughters at our property, a decade or so prior to our arrival, and that this was the reason for the grand upgrade of our property. Inside our front door is a welcoming vestibule with a marble fireplace, and to one side of this foyer is a cloakroom and a guest toilet. Architect Sir Michael Fowler and the Tolhursts designed this luxurious use of space for guests, and it is something I have never contemplated changing as it works so well. The Tolhurst wedding was held in a marquee and the catering was undertaken by Joe Walding, who owned a catering company at the time in Palmerston North. He later became a Cabinet Minister in the 1972–75 Labour government.

In the summer, there is a wedding at Springfield nearly every Saturday, and brides in all shapes and sizes, nationalities and denominations have become a regular feature of Springfield life. Sometimes the bride and groom choose St Margaret's church at the top of the driveway for their ceremony or sometimes the gazebo in our garden, or even one of our glorious trees may have a particular significance for them. Bridal parties have been known to vanish with their guests to the beach or up into the bush for the wedding vows. And no guest has ever taken liberties with household objects or precious ornaments.

On a warm summer's evening, small weddings can be seated outside at one long table. If the weather is inclement on the day we move into our sitting-room, where sitting-room furniture is replaced with dining furniture. And the covered decks around the house are perfect for pre-dinner drinks or ceremonies that were planned for outdoors.

Sophie, our French poodle, always enjoys a wedding, and preens herself in preparation for the photographs. She is a very vain dog and will stand proudly in front of the wedding group, facing the camera.

Every wedding couple brings a uniqueness to their special day, and I am continually amazed by the points of difference. The dynamics change with every group – it may be a groom who weeps with happiness when he turns to see his bride, a grandmother who has a little too much bubbly in the sun and collapses on our bed, the little girl whose highlight at the wedding is helping me, or the reunification of two family members previously at loggerheads.

Weddings are glowing brides, handsome grooms, glamorous gowns, scented flowers, extraordinary cakes and well-dressed guests. More than that though, weddings are days filled with emotion, love and happiness, and I feel proud that people want to spend this special day in my home.

In the summer, there is a wedding at Springfield nearly every Saturday, and brides in all shapes and sizes, nationalities and denominations have become a regular feature of Springfield life.

Pacific Oysters on the Half-shell with
Balsamic Vinegar and Lemons

Photograph: James Gilbert

Pacific Oysters on the Half-shell with Balsamic Vinegar and Lemons

SERVES 30

10–30 dozen Pacific oysters
   in the half-shell

ice

balsamic vinegar

lemons

Maldon sea salt and freshly
   ground black pepper

Soft White Dinner Rolls
   (see page 116)

+ *The ultimate, no-work hors d'oeuvre.*

+ Allow 4–12 Pacific oysters in the half-shell per guest, depending on your generosity, the volume of the meal to follow, or how many oyster lovers you predict will be in your group.

+ Fill a deep tray, garden urn, or half barrel with ice and, just before guests arrive, cover ice with oysters in the half-shell.

+ Accompany oysters with the best bottle of balsamic vinegar you can find or your budget will allow, a bucket of lemon halves, and salt and pepper grinders. Small, Soft White Dinner Rolls presented with a bowl of herbed butter would also be appreciated.

+ Provide guests with side plates, cocktail forks and a big empty bucket to put the shells in.

Tuna Tartare with Japanese Rice Sprinkles

MAKES 15–20 COCKTAIL SERVES

300g tuna fillet (skin on, bone out)

1 tube wasabi paste

1 packet (30g) Japanese Rice Sprinkles

100ml Tamari soy sauce

+ *My friend Mark Limacher, chef/owner of Roxburgh Bistro in Wellington, gave me this idea. It is wonderful to do at home because it is so simple. If the tuna is good quality and very fresh you will receive endless compliments, and it is fabulous with champagne. You will find Japanese Rice Sprinkles in an Asian supply shop. (The photo of the sprinkles on top of rice in a bowl on the front of the packet will indicate you are buying the correct product.)*

+ Trim tuna and cut into bite-sized cubes, approximately 3cm square.

+ Just before you serve, thinly spread wasabi paste all over cubes until evenly coated.

+ Roll cubes in Japanese Rice Sprinkles to coat.

+ Skewer cubes on toothpicks and arrange on a serving platter.

+ Serve Tuna Tartare with Tamari soy sauce for dipping.

←
Smoked Duck Breast Salad with Roasted
Peaches and Tarragon Dressing

Smoked Duck Breast Salad with Roasted Peaches and Tarragon Dressing

SERVES 8 AS AN ENTRÉE

1.12kg (4) duck breasts

Brine (for Smoked Duck)
   (see below)

Roasted Peaches
   (see page 171)

8 large handfuls of small rocket
   leaves, or baby salad
   greens

Tarragon Dressing
   (see page 171)

+ *Duck is a special occasion meat and makes an appreciated change from chicken or red meat. A home smoker is relatively inexpensive to buy and can be purchased at most kitchen shops. This is a terrific entrée and very befitting a wedding feast.*

+ With a sharp knife criss-cross duck skin.

+ To render fat from duck, place duck skin-side down, in a hot dry pan, then pour off fat as it comes out of duck. Keep fat for another use.

+ When fat under the skin has diminished by about half, remove duck from the pan and cool.

+ Place Brine into a bowl, add duck breast and place in refrigerator for a minimum of 6 hours or overnight.

+ Drain off Brine and pat duck breast dry with a paper towel.

+ Place duck breast into a prepared smoker and cook for 12–15 minutes or until duck is cooked medium-rare.

+ Remove from smoker and leave to cool. You can prepare to this stage up to 2 days ahead.

+ To serve, slice duck breast thinly on the diagonal.

+ Place a piece of Roasted Peach in the centre of 8 large dinner plates with the sliced duck next to it. Nestle a handful of rocket or baby salad greens next to peach.

+ Drizzle each portion of duck and salad with a tablespoon of Tarragon Dressing. Serve immediately.

MAKES 1.350 LITRES

65g (½ cup) Maldon sea salt

65g (5 tblsp + 1 tsp) brown
   sugar

1.25 litres (5 cups) water

Brine (for Smoked Duck)

+ Combine all ingredients in a large bowl or jug.

+ Stir until salt and sugar is dissolved.

←
Wedding buffet

Roasted Peaches

MAKES 8 SERVES

350–400g (2) fresh peaches

+ *Roasting intensifies the flavour and softens the fruit for use in a salad. In winter try this technique with pears, which can be used in place of peaches in the Smoked Duck Salad recipe.*

+ Preheat oven to 190°C.

+ Cut peaches in half and using a melon baller remove the stones.

+ Cut halves into 2 or 3 pieces lengthwise.

+ Grease a roasting pan lightly and place peaches in pan sitting on cut edges.

+ Roast for 7–8 minutes. Remove pan from oven and turn peaches over onto the second cut edge.

+ Return to oven and roast a further 7–8 minutes until peaches are tender but still retain their shape. Roasting time will vary according to ripeness.

MAKES 120ML

75ml (5 tblsp) olive oil

15ml (1 tblsp) red wine vinegar

2 tblsp Dijon mustard

1 tblsp chopped French tarragon

¼ tsp Maldon sea salt

¼ tsp freshly ground black pepper

Tarragon Dressing

+ *I also enjoy this dressing with roasted beetroot, or over cold chicken.*

+ Place all ingredients in a bowl and, using an electric hand-held blender or a whisk, whisk until ingredients are emulsified.

←

Spit-roasted Suckling Pig with Apple
Sauce and Tamarillo Chutney

Spit-roasted Suckling Pig with Apple Sauce and Tamarillo Chutney

SERVES 20–25 OR 25–30

12–15kg suckling pig
  (prepared for spit roasting)

bunches of rosemary
  and thyme

500ml (2 cups) cream

Apple Sauce
  (see page 186)

Tamarillo Chutney
  (see page 187)

+ *In a buffet situation where you are serving one meat only, the lower weight of suckling pig serves 20–25 guests and the upper weight serves 25–30 guests. Hire a spit from your local hireage company, but remember to book ahead. I use a spit with an electric motor but a gas flame. Ask your butcher to prepare the pig ready for spit roasting.*

+ Loosely stuff stomach cavity of pig with rosemary and thyme.

+ Push spit rod through one end of pig to the other.

+ Using a larding needle, stitch up pig stomach cavity with wire.

+ Place pig on spit and brush outside of pig with cream. Turn spit up to high and rotate pig for 30 minutes.

+ Reduce temperature of spit and cook pig for a further 2½–3 hours, basting regularly with cream. Test with a metal skewer, or better still with a meat thermometer, for readiness.

+ With the spit turned off, rest pig for at least 30 minutes, loosely covered with heavy towels to retain heat. Resting is very important as it will relax the meat which makes carving easier and will provide a larger portion yield.

+ Remove pig from spit and place on a very large board or dedicated table. Remove spit rod, cut wire and pull wire out.

+ Lay the pig on its side and carve onto guests' plates or onto communal platters. The correct way to carve a whole animal is to cut into body parts as you go, i.e. cut off a leg, then carve the leg.

+ Serve with Apple Sauce and Tamarillo Chutney.

→
Salad of Baby
Spinach with Sweet
and Sour Balsamic
Roasted Onions

Salad of Baby Spinach with Sweet and Sour Balsamic Roasted Onions

SERVES 8

240g fresh baby spinach

Sweet and Sour Balsamic Roasted Onions (see below)

Maldon sea salt and freshly ground pepper

Balsamic Vinaigrette (see below)

sunflower petals to garnish

+ *My friend and colleague Shelley Templer, who owns Kauri Catering in Brussels, gave me this salad recipe of which I am particularly fond. It is best assembled as close to serving time as possible.*

+ Wash and drain baby spinach. I like to remove water with a salad spinner.

+ Pile spinach on a serving platter. Scatter hot Sweet and Sour Roasted Balsamic Onions over spinach and season to taste.

+ Drizzle with Balsamic Vinaigrette and garnish with sunflower petals.

+ Serve immediately.

Sweet and Sour Balsamic Roasted Onions

SERVES 8

430g (4 large) red onions (peeled and cut into wedges through the root)

60ml (¼ cup) olive oil

40ml (2 tblsp + 2 tsp) balsamic vinegar

30g (2½ tblsp) brown sugar

salt and freshly ground black pepper

+ *If you wish you can prepare the onions ahead and then reheat to add to salad.*

+ Preheat oven to 180°C. Combine onions with remaining ingredients and spread out in a single layer in a non-reactive, shallow roasting dish.

+ Roast onions for 35–40 minutes or until tender and beginning to brown at edges. Use immediately or allow to cool. Cover and refrigerate until required.

Balsamic Vinaigrette

SERVES 8

45ml (3 tblsp) balsamic vinegar (the best one that you can afford)

135ml (½ cup + 2 tsp) extra virgin olive oil

¼ tsp Maldon sea salt (or to taste)

freshly ground black pepper to taste

+ Combine all ingredients in a non-reactive bowl and mix well. Cover until required.

←
Green Bean, Black
Olive and Mint Salad

Green Bean, Black Olive and Mint Salad

SERVES 6–8

600g green beans

pinch salt

100g black olives

olive-infused extra virgin
   olive oil

handful of mint leaves
   (chopped)

Maldon sea salt and freshly
   ground black pepper

+ *Sue Sue grows the nicest beans I have ever tasted. Occasionally I will combine her green beans with butterbeans, or even use only butterbeans. When I open a can of olives, I drain off the brine, rinse, then place them in a jar and cover with extra virgin olive oil. I call this olive-infused extra virgin olive oil and save it to brush on crostini, or to use in dressings.*

+ Prepare beans. With round beans I just take the stalk end off and for flat beans I pull through a bean slicer to end up with thinly sliced beans.

+ Bring a medium saucepan of water to the boil. Add a pinch of salt and beans, and cook beans until al dente. Drain and proceed with salad while they are still warm, or chill until you are ready to make salad.

+ Place the beans on a platter and scatter with black olives. Drizzle with olive-infused extra virgin olive oil, sprinkle with mint and season.

→

Cos Lettuce and
Orange Salad

SERVES 10

10 generous handfuls cos
   lettuce leaves

5 oranges (peeled and
   segmented; save juice
   for dressing)

Orange Vinaigrette (see below)

a handful of heartsease
   (pansies)

Cos Lettuce and Orange Salad

+ *This is a refreshing, colourful salad. In a different context I might add toasted pinenuts and sliced avocados.*

+ Pile lettuce leaves on a large platter and scatter orange segments over the top.

+ Drizzle with Orange Vinaigrette and sprinkle with heartsease.

Orange Vinaigrette

MAKES 200ML

125ml (½ cup) extra virgin
   olive oil

7.5ml (½ tblsp) balsamic
   vinegar

62.5ml (¼ cup) fresh orange
   juice

finely grated zest of 1 orange

½ tsp Maldon sea salt

freshly ground black pepper

+ Whisk all ingredients in a non-reactive bowl.

← Lemon and Almond Tart

→ Peter Robson at Windsor Park picks raspberries daily for his shop

Lemon and Almond Tart with Fresh Raspberries and Vanilla Bean Ice-cream

SERVES 8

½ recipe Lemon and Almond
   Tart Pastry
   (see page 182)

1 egg white (lightly beaten)

1 recipe Lemon and Almond
   Tart Filling (see page 182)

fresh raspberries

Vanilla Bean Ice-cream
   (see page 183)

icing sugar to dust

+ *This particular lemon tart recipe is more durable than a benchmark one. It can be made several days ahead, or even baked and frozen, so it's perfect for entertaining.*

+ Preheat oven to 200°C. Spray a 24cm flan tin with baking spray.

+ On a lightly floured bench, roll out pastry to 2mm thickness and line the tin. Paint pastry base with egg white.

+ Pour filling into the unbaked tart shell and bake in the centre of the oven for 30–40 minutes, or until light golden brown and set.

+ Remove from oven and cool, or refrigerate until ready to serve.

+ Dust tart with icing sugar and serve with fresh raspberries and Vanilla Bean Ice-cream.

Lemon and Almond Tart Pastry

*MAKES ENOUGH PASTRY FOR
2 24CM TARTS*

160g (1 cup + 3 tblsp) flour

50g (5 tblsp) castor sugar

35g (6 tblsp) ground almonds

zest of 1 lemon

pinch of salt

115g butter (finely diced
    and chilled)

1 egg

1 tsp rum

1 tsp milk

+ *Freeze half the pastry until you are ready to make another tart or use as a firm base for other pie fillings. It's a very tasty pastry for Christmas Mince Pies or a strong pastry for a baked cheesecake.*

+ Place flour, sugar, ground almonds, lemon zest and salt in a food processor with a metal blade fitted.

+ Sprinkle butter over flour mixture and process until mixture resembles breadcrumbs.

+ In a small jug whisk together egg, rum and milk. With the food processor running, pour egg mixture through feed tube until the pastry just begins to form a ball (you may not need to add all of the liquid). Remove pastry from the food processor and press into a disc.

+ Divide pastry into 2 equal balls, wrap each in plastic wrap and chill for at least 30 minutes or overnight in the refrigerator. Alternatively, freeze.

Lemon and Almond Tart Filling

*MAKES ENOUGH FILLING FOR
1 24CM TART*

3 eggs

165g (¾ cup + 1 tblsp) castor
    sugar

zest of 3 lemons

juice of 3 lemons (75ml)

115g (1 cup) ground almonds

140g butter (softened to
    almost melting)

+ *For this filling use the food processor just to combine the ingredients, but don't mix to the stage where the filling has froth. It is critical to this recipe that the butter is almost melted rather than totally melted.*

+ Place eggs, sugar, lemon zest, lemon juice and ground almonds in a food processor fitted with a metal blade and process until just blended but not frothy.

+ With the food processor running, slowly pour butter from a jug through the feed tube and process until the mixture has amalgamated. Taste for lemon and, if necessary, add more lemon juice.

→

Vanilla Bean Ice-cream

Vanilla Bean Ice-cream

MAKES 900ML (SERVES 5–6 GENEROUSLY)

100g sugar

75ml water

1 vanilla bean
(split in half lengthways)

4 egg yolks

300ml cream
(lightly whipped)

+ Place sugar, water and vanilla bean into a small saucepan over a medium-low heat and stir until sugar is dissolved.

+ Bring to the boil and simmer for approximately 17 minutes or until the syrup has small, even-sized bubbles all the way across the pot (108°C/220°F on a sugar thermometer).

+ Place egg yolks into an electric mixer and whisk for 1 minute.

+ Remove syrup from heat and allow to sit for 30 seconds. Remove the vanilla bean (wash, dry and store for future use).

+ Gradually pour the hot sugar syrup in the bowl with egg yolks, whisking continuously (you will need to scrape down the sides of the bowl to prevent the build-up of syrup).

+ Continue whisking until the mixture has cooled, at which stage it will be whitish in colour and double its original volume.

+ Fold whipped cream into the egg mixture and pour into a container with a lid suitable for the freezer. Freeze overnight or for up to 1 week.

LARDER

Old Mother Hubbard
went to the cupboard
to get her poor dog a bone,
when she got there
the cupboard was bare
and so the poor dog had none

She went to the tavern
for white wine and red
but when she came back
the dog stood on his head

She went to the baker's
to buy him some bread
but when she came back
the poor dog was dead

In my restaurant days, I always had an empty fridge and absolutely nothing in the cupboards at home. Paul, whom I met in his furniture removal days when he came to my house for a removal, loves telling people that the only cupboard he found something in was the drinks' cupboard. The fridge had a quarter of a cabbage and half a carton of sour milk.

I've moved on since then, and now I appreciate and enjoy all my creature comforts at home. People often ask me who cooks and what do we eat when we are home alone. The answer is that I always cook when we are entertaining, but for the two of us, or when James visits, either Paul or I cook – whoever feels like it really.

We cook very simple food; it can be grilled fish with rice, steak with beans, roast chicken with kumara or pasta with herbs.

of feta cheese for tasty tapas and, as we are an hour's drive from a good bread shop, there has to be good bread in the freezer. Then there are the things for the larder that I make myself. If I'm making short pastry for a tart, I'll always make a second ball for the freezer. If I have abundant herbs in the garden, I will turn them into herb butter or chicken stuffing for the freezer, or infuse oil to use for drizzling or painting on food.

I don't go overboard on making jams, jellies and preserves, but I will always make a few jars of things that have proved useful in the past. It's quite simple sometimes to make one or two jars of a favourite chutney while you are waiting for dinner to cook.

With a little planning ahead it is easy to make your everyday eating more interesting – and your entertaining more streamlined.

And I always like to buy my meat, vegetables and fruit fresh; just a small amount every day or two. However, I do rely heavily on my larder, because if all else fails I can whip up something tasty from what's on hand.

There are some musts I would never be without – Italian dried pasta and tinned tuna in oil for a start; jasmine rice is always in the cupboard, and garlic, ginger and red chillies in the fridge or freezer. A block of Parmesan cheese is a must, and a small selection of extra virgin olive oils, backed up by two or three grades of balsamic vinegar, which go a long way to making something great out of something simple. Bacon and sliced prosciutto, and a few punnets of home-made chicken stock are not to be sniffed at in the fridge or freezer. Two or three different types of olives are perfect with a small block

Sweet Short Pastry

MAKES ONE BALL

200g (1 cup + ⅓ cup
 + 1 tblsp) flour

½ tsp salt

30g (3 tblsp) sugar

100g unsalted butter (finely
 diced)

1 egg yolk

45ml (3 tblsp) cold water
 (approximately)

+ *This pastry freezes really well so if you are making one to use,
 make another to freeze.*

+ Place flour, salt and sugar into a food processor fitted with a metal blade.

+ Sprinkle butter over flour.

+ Process flour and butter mixture until it resembles fine breadcrumbs.

+ In a small bowl, whisk egg yolk with cold water.

+ With the food processor running, pour egg yolk and water through the
 feed tube. Continue to process until the pastry forms a ball and sits above
 the blade of the machine.

+ If the pastry does not form a ball easily, remove mixture from food
 processor and finish the balling process with your hands. To continue
 in the food processor will toughen the pastry.

+ Knead pastry into a disc shape, wrap in plastic wrap and rest for at least
 30 minutes in the fridge before using.

Short Pastry

+ *Use the same ingredients and method as Sweet Short Pastry,
 except delete the sugar and replace with ½ teaspoon of freshly
 ground black pepper. If you are making pastry ahead, either to
 store in the refrigerator or freezer, then use freshly ground white
 pepper as black pepper can 'bleed' into the pastry.*

Apple Sauce

MAKES 375ML

3 (about 500g) Granny Smith
 apples (peeled and cored)

30ml (2 tblsp) brandy

1 cinnamon stick

15g (1 tblsp) sugar

250ml (1 cup) water

½ tsp freshly grated nutmeg

Maldon sea salt and freshly
 ground pepper

+ *Granny Smith apples produce a smooth apple sauce, but if
 you prefer a chunky apple sauce then use Braeburn apples.*

+ Roughly chop apples and place in a non-reactive pot.

+ Add brandy, cinnamon stick, sugar and water and bring to the boil.

+ Simmer for 8–10 minutes, stirring occasionally, until the apples are
 soft and the juices have evaporated.

+ Beat with a wooden spoon until smooth. Add nutmeg and season
 to taste. Serve warm.

Tamarillo Chutney

+ *This recipe is adapted from* The Essential Digby Law *published by Hodder Moa Beckett. It is the queen of fruit chutneys and the preserve I make the most after Tomato Chilli Jam.*

MAKES 2 LITRES

1.75kg tamarillos (peeled and chopped)

750g apples (peeled, cored and chopped)

500g onions (peeled and chopped)

600ml malt vinegar

1 tblsp salt

1½ tsp mustard powder

1 tsp mixed spice

1kg brown sugar

+ Combine all ingredients in a large non-reactive saucepan, and bring to the boil.

+ Simmer very gently for about 2 hours, stirring often.

+ Pour into hot, clean jars and seal.

Worcestershire Sauce

+ *This recipe is also adapted from* The Essential Digby Law, *published by Hodder Moa Beckett. It's great to add to sauces and gravies, and is excellent on pies and oysters.*

MAKES 300ML

315ml (1¼ cups) malt vinegar

250g (¾ cup) treacle

1 tsp salt

¾cm root ginger (peeled and finely chopped)

1 clove garlic (finely chopped)

1½ tsp ground cloves

¼ tsp cayenne pepper

+ Combine all ingredients in a non-reactive saucepan. Bring to the boil, then turn heat down and simmer gently for 20 minutes.

+ Cover and let stand overnight at room temperature.

+ The following day, strain sauce through a fine sieve covered with muslin and pour into bottles.

+ The sauce is ready to use immediately or can be stored, covered in a cool room for up to one year. Shake before each use.

Raspberry Jam

MAKES 3¾ 300ML JARS

1kg raspberries
1kg sugar
a knob of butter

+ *This is the largest quantity of raspberry jam I make in one pot. With all jams, jellies or chutneys, the colour and flavour significantly decrease when made in large quantities. Raspberry Jam is handy for puddings; children love it in sandwiches and I enjoy it on toast for breakfast.*

+ Place raspberries in a non-reactive saucepan and cook slowly until juices run from the raspberries (approximately 7 minutes).

+ Add sugar and stir until dissolved. Boil rapidly for approximately 30 minutes.

+ Test for setting by placing a small amount of jam on a saucer and place in the freezer for 1 minute. If a thick skin forms on the jam, the jam is ready.

+ Remove scum from the top of the jam. Add butter to enrich and give gloss to the final product.

+ Pour into sterilised jars and seal.

Vogel's Toast Rounds

MAKES 46 VOGEL'S TOAST ROUNDS

23 slices medium Vogel's
     bread

+ *These are very crisp, and make an excellent vehicle for dips and spreads.*

+ Preheat oven to 150ºC. With a 5cm cookie cutter, cut each slice of Vogel's into 2 rounds.

+ Place rounds on baking tray and bake for 40 minutes or until bread is browned and dry.

+ When cool, store in an airtight container for up to 4 days or freeze until required.

Orange Syrup

ENOUGH FOR 123CM BAKLAVA

150g (¾ cup) sugar
200ml (¾ cup + 1 tblsp) water
60g (4 tblsp) honey
90ml (6 tblsp) orange juice
zest of one orange

+ In a small saucepan combine sugar, water, honey, orange juice and zest.

+ Place over a medium heat and stir until sugar is dissolved.

+ Bring to the boil, turn the heat down and simmer very gently for 5 minutes until syrupy.

+ Remove from heat and allow to cool.

Mint or Basil Pesto

MAKES 425ML

1 cup mint or basil leaves
(tightly packed)
125ml (½ cup) lemon juice
1 cup pinenuts
1½ tsp salt
125ml (½ cup) olive oil

+ *I like pesto without cheese or garlic as you can really taste the freshness of the herb. Make during summer and freeze to enjoy during winter.*

+ Place mint or basil and lemon juice in the bowl of a food processor fitted with a metal blade and process to chop.

+ Add pinenuts and salt, and process until well blended. With the motor running, drizzle in olive oil to form a smooth paste. Taste for seasoning.

Basic Mayonnaise

MAKES 562.5ML

4 egg yolks
Maldon sea salt and freshly
ground pepper
juice of one lemon
500ml (2 cups) salad oil

+ *This is very useful to have on hand for a myriad uses. Ban commercial mayonnaise from your larder totally.*

+ Place egg yolks, salt, pepper, lemon juice and ¼ cup salad oil in a food processor fitted with a metal blade. Blend until smooth.

+ Very slowly, pour remaining salad oil through the feed tube with food processor running. Season to taste.

+ If the mayonnaise is too thick, thin down with 1 tblsp boiling water slowly poured through the feed tube.

+ Keep covered in the fridge for up to 10 days.

MAKES 375ML

2 egg yolks
1 clove garlic (peeled)
½ tblsp mild mustard
1 tblsp lemon juice
50ml (3 tblsp + 1 tsp) lime
juice (3–4 limes juiced)
1 tblsp lime zest
250ml (1 cup) salad oil
½ tsp Maldon sea salt
¼ tsp freshly ground black
pepper

Lime Mayonnaise

+ *For Lemon Mayonnaise, substitute lemon juice and zest for lime.*

+ Place egg yolks, garlic, mustard, lemon juice, lime juice, zest and ¼ cup salad oil in a food processor fitted with a metal blade. Blend until smooth.

+ With the food processor running, pour remaining salad oil very slowly through the feed tube until all of the oil is combined. Season to taste.

+ Keep covered in the fridge for up to a week. If kept, taste again before you use.

INDEX

I am very grateful to my friend Murray Lloyd, my photographer for this book. Murray and I spent many creative days working at Springfield – with me cooking and styling the food for the photographs, and Murray working hard to achieve a look that epitomized Springfield.

A big thank you to Chef Jo-Anne Tracey who very scientifically tested and retested all the recipes. I feel confident that home cooks will be able to cook from this book with ease.

Thank you to Nicolette Gregory who put together the manuscript, and to Pauline Graham, our catering kitchen manager, who allowed me the time to concentrate on a project such as this. Thank you to Clare Douglas, our gardener, who like me thrives on colourful bold gardens, but unlike me does all the hard work.

Thank you to my family (especially Paul) and friends who feature in the photographs included in the book. Thank you to the colleagues who allowed me to use some of their recipes. Thank you to Bernice Beachman and Philippa Gerrard at Penguin – for their inspiration and patience. Thank you to Paul Shadbolt at Seven for giving me everything I wanted, including my beautiful endpapers. And thank you to Springfield for being what it is.